2019
外汇贵金属行业发展蓝皮书
（中国及东南亚市场）

FX168金融研究院　编

上海财经大学出版社

图书在版编目(CIP)数据

2019外汇贵金属行业发展蓝皮书：中国及东南亚市场/FX168金融研究院编．—上海：上海财经大学出版社，2020.5

ISBN 978-7-5642-3509-3/F·3509

Ⅰ.①2… Ⅱ.①F… Ⅲ.①外汇市场-研究报告-中国-2019②贵金属-投资-研究报告-中国-2019③外汇市场-研究报告-东南亚-2019④贵金属-投资-研究报告-东南亚-2019 Ⅳ.①F832.5②F833.305

中国版本图书馆CIP数据核字(2020)第056187号

□ 责任编辑　李志浩

2019外汇贵金属行业发展蓝皮书(中国及东南亚市场)
FX168金融研究院　编

上海财经大学出版社出版发行
(上海市中山北一路369号　邮编200083)
网　　址：http://www.sufep.com
电子邮箱：webmaster@sufep.com
全国新华书店经销
北京虎彩文化传播有限公司印刷装订
2020年5月第1版　2020年5月第1次印刷

889mm×1194mm　1/16　13印张　261千字
定价：168.00元

《2019 外汇贵金属行业发展蓝皮书》
（中国及东南亚市场）

编委会主任

江　泰

执行编辑

梅菊桃　李　莎

编　　辑

程　越　邵　星　宋　南　汤擎天　张文娟

编委会成员

安虎生　方丽娟　郭永生　杭　帆　何　扬　季晓明
钱海翔　沈婷燕　王晓竹　郁　欣　周　莉

校　　对

宁宇骁

封面设计

王佳蕊

编辑说明

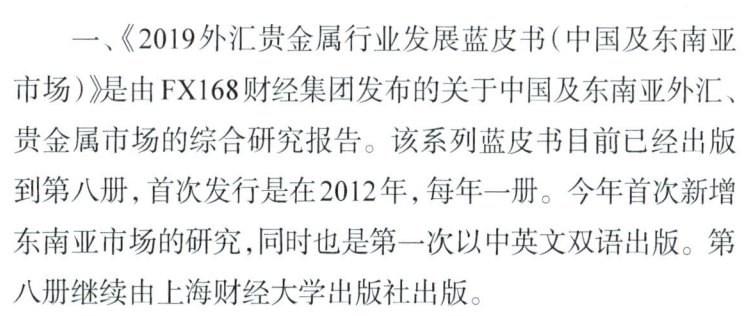

一、《2019外汇贵金属行业发展蓝皮书（中国及东南亚市场）》是由FX168财经集团发布的关于中国及东南亚外汇、贵金属市场的综合研究报告。该系列蓝皮书目前已经出版到第八册，首次发行是在2012年，每年一册。今年首次新增东南亚市场的研究，同时也是第一次以中英文双语出版。第八册继续由上海财经大学出版社出版。

二、本书共分为六个部分：第一部分综述全球外汇及加密货币行业热点与趋势，第二部分为中国及东南亚零售外汇市场投资者结构及行为分析，第三部分人民币外汇期货及人民币汇率，第四部分是全球主要交易所2019年发展情况，第五部分为东南亚市场营商环境及行业现状的研究，第六部分附录。

三、本书内容和数据均由FX168财经集团通过公开渠道、自身运营数据、第三方合作机构提供、外部邀稿采集、编辑，数据力求真实有效。

四、蓝皮书在编辑过程中，得到各金融机构、高校学者和个人投资者的大力支持和协助，在此一并致谢。

《2019外汇贵金属行业发展蓝皮书
（中国及东南亚市场）》编委会
2020年3月

序

在《2019外汇贵金属行业发展蓝皮书（中国及东南亚市场）》出版之际，本人有感而发。主要感触是全球为了推迟金融危机的爆发，主要经济体又启动了宽松量化的货币政策QE，那些原本要爬出"流动性陷阱"的国家又重新跌入"流动性陷阱"，零利率和负利率又变成"常态"，没有国库券背书的货币发行似乎难以避免，由此，全球游资势必流向房地产和股市，进一步推高原来就高企的"泡沫"。此外，避险货币、黄金等贵金属也成为"投机"关注的对象。

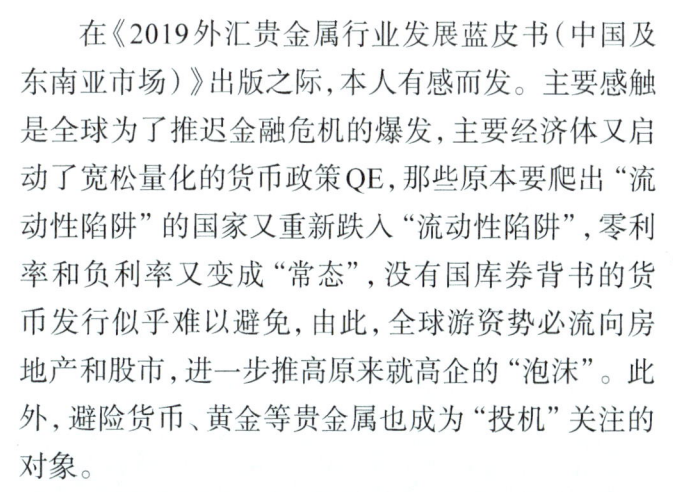

本蓝皮书回顾了2019年外汇和贵金属行业的热点和趋势，并对2020年进行展望。

自从中国人民币加入了SDR后，五种货币由于互相参照，近几年来的趋同性更加明显。在几种货币中，日元相对稍有些"个性"，这与日元变成了全球的"避险货币"因素有关。

美元在2019年的水平上2020年继续向上乏力。欧元则是美元的对照物，有望低位反弹。英镑则夹在欧元与美元之间，并与脱欧是否顺利相关。人民币汇率仍然受到中美贸易摩擦激化与缓和，以及新冠肺炎疫情发展的影响而宽幅震荡。

黄金与贵金属商品价格不仅继续受到QE的影响总体向上，而且受到地缘政治的影响而宽度波动。其他贵金属价格还取决于世界经济是否回暖因素的影响。全球都关注着科技革命在关键领域的爆发，尤其是人工智能、大数据、区块链在实体经济和金融领域的运用。科技革命可以改变各种价格轨迹。

2020年是不确定因素较多的一年。因为各种"窗口"都开启着，诸如金融危机或科技革命爆发都有可能。做好各种应对措施才是硬道理。

丁剑平

上海财经大学现代金融研究中心主任、教授（博导）

序

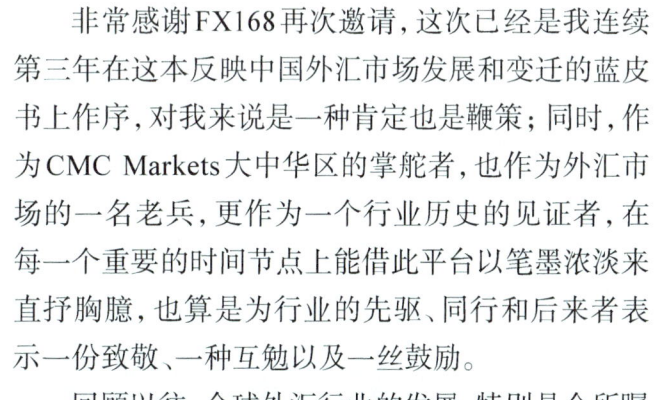

非常感谢FX168再次邀请，这次已经是我连续第三年在这本反映中国外汇市场发展和变迁的蓝皮书上作序，对我来说是一种肯定也是鞭策；同时，作为CMC Markets大中华区的掌舵者，也作为外汇市场的一名老兵，更作为一个行业历史的见证者，在每一个重要的时间节点上能借此平台以笔墨浓淡来直抒胸臆，也算是为行业的先驱、同行和后来者表示一份致敬、一种互勉以及一丝鼓励。

回顾以往，全球外汇行业的发展，特别是众所瞩目的零售外汇市场的发展已经走到了一个十字路口。是继续前行、左右彷徨还是匆匆离开，成为每一个外汇人职业生涯中的关键命题。如果是选择继续前行，自身内在商业模式的调整在外部监管大环境的严厉调控下如何做到相得益彰，将会是在这条产业链上脱颖而出的决胜关键，而不是仅仅依靠游离在主流监管体系外的权宜之计来获得喘息之机。因为缺乏强力有效的监管机制，安全、专业和透明这些金融行业中必不可少的注脚将会显得那么苍白无力。如果在困难和压力中踌躇不前，左右彷徨，失去了应有的锐意进取的精神，再加上过去陈旧的以量

变为主的运营模式正在经受着行业新常态的不断冲击，使得逆流行舟之下不但有着倒退而被淘汰的风险，更有浪打船翻的可能。最后，因一时的艰难和无法适应而选择黯然退场或转战他方，成为生态圈中物竞天择的牺牲品，更是有一种"壮志未酬"的无奈和遗憾。

展望未来，外汇和其衍生产品始终是国际主流金融市场中不可或缺的一部分，无论是机构还是个人对于此类产品的需求都是呈现着快速增长的态势。作为行业中的专业人士，如何更好地正确引导客户的需求，将其转化为监管机制所认可的业务模式，是为发展的前途正道。这是一个复杂的沟通、交流、探讨和实践的过程，也随时存在着半途中推倒重来的可能，但这并不妨碍从业者、客户和监管在这个过程中树立起各自领域应有的信心。从业者将会在这去芜存菁的过程中不断淬炼自身的专业能力，让其代表的外汇行业的形象逐渐与主流金融行业相融合；而客户则能在这个过程中逐步提升自身的认知水平和风险承受能力，形成独立的判断能力，从而避免掉入各种陷阱；监管则能从这个过程中进一步了解产业链和商业模式，来提高自身的管理水平和理念，为能够进一步引导这个行业的良性发展增强信心。

在此序的最后，我深信虽然时代的变迁如同大浪淘沙，而精华将永远矗立在那儿不动不摇。

CMC Markets 大中华区总裁
2020年2月17日

CMC Markets 为全球领先的在线交易和机构平台技术解决方案供应商，成立于1989年，拥有30年历史，是全球首个发布零售在线外汇交易平台的交易提供商。市场范围涵盖全球15个国家国际市场，为全球超过8万活跃客户提供外汇、股票、股指、债券以及大宗商品等五大资产类别近万种金融产品。作为伦敦证券交易所（LSE）上市公司，CMC Markets 接受多国政府监管机构监管。

序

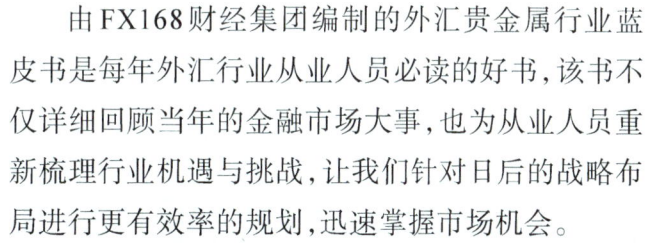

　　由FX168财经集团编制的外汇贵金属行业蓝皮书是每年外汇行业从业人员必读的好书,该书不仅详细回顾当年的金融市场大事,也为从业人员重新梳理行业机遇与挑战,让我们针对日后的战略布局进行更有效率的规划,迅速掌握市场机会。

　　2019年对中国外汇行业来说是充满变化的一年,而我们也一同见证了许多重要时刻,如中国国家外汇管理局取消合格境外机构投资者(QFII)和人民币合格境外机构投资者(RQFII)之投资额度限制等,而在外汇相关政策逐渐松绑的趋势下,未来人民币将持续走向国际,同时提升外资跨境参与市场之便利性,为市场提供充足的流动性。

　　今年的蓝皮书比起过去特别增加了东南亚市场的分析。说到这,KVB PRIME要在这里特别感谢FX168邀请我们参加2019西贡交易博览(SFES),并在活动的闭门会议上为KVB PRIME详细分享和介绍越南当地的经商环境、在越南本地开展业务需要注意的相关事项,同时也为我们提供与当地投资者进行面对面交流的机会,让我们对东南

1

亚的战略布局以及用户需求有了更清晰的认识。

　　近年来，东南亚经济快速增长、基础设施条件持续改善，在这些关键因素刺激下，东南亚已成为各家交易商的发展首选。KVB PRIME 2019年除了受邀出席有上千名投资者到访参加的2019西贡交易博览（SFES），还在越南及马来西亚主办投资研讨会，吸引数百位投资者现场参会，可见东南亚市场的发展潜力惊人。

　　未来，在中国外汇政策逐渐开放以及东南亚市场崛起的趋势下，外汇行业的发展前景可期，相信只要每年追随FX168所制作的蓝皮书，我们对于未来的金融市场及行业趋势将会有更深入的了解。

KVB PRIME英国市场部经理

　　KVB PRIME 为投资者提供卓越的金融服务，让投资者享受极具优势的交易成本和流畅的交易体验。KVB PRIME 所提供的卓越服务在全球各大金融展会荣获大奖，包括最佳交易执行经纪商、亚太区最具影响力经纪商等。

目 录

序 .... 丁剑平　1
序 .... 程必逸　1
序 .... Olivia Cheng　1

第1部分　全球外汇及加密货币行业热点与趋势

（一）2019年全球外汇市场热点 2
　　1. 日元闪崩拉开2019年序幕　日本STP经纪商受损严重 2
　　2. 外汇行业面临跨境联合监管　ASIC及香港证监会警告发牌机构 3
　　3. 中国继续强调跨境金融服务监管风险　再度点名外汇保证金交易 4
　　4. 全球监管进一步收紧　差价合约交易杠杆被大幅下调 5
　　5. 营商环境恶化　英国券商SVSFX、AFX Markets先后宣布破产 6
　　6. CFTC过去一年各大经纪商运营数据：OANDA安达追平嘉盛 6
　　7. 上海第十七届理财博览会如期举办　外汇展商数量锐减 10
　　8. FX168点评旗舰店舆情监控指数显示经纪商市场口碑还有提升空间 10
　　9. 2019财年经纪商面临的挑战和机遇 11

1

（二）2019年全球加密货币市场热点 14
1. 脸书Libra面世困难重重　监管层疑虑众多难以放行 14
2. 中国央行法定数字货币呼之欲出　2020是中国法定数字货币元年？ 15
3. 亚洲各国对加密货币态度不一　中国仍然最严格 16
（三）中国外汇市场发展大事记（2019年） 18

第2部分　中国及东南亚零售外汇市场投资者结构及行为分析

（一）中国地区 22
1. 中国投资者中男性为绝对主力，其中一家社区的数据显示男性占比极高 22
2. 中国投资者中25—34岁年龄段为主力，第二主力年龄段不同平台有所分化 ... 23
3. 中国投资者最为集中的是广东省，湖北省用户占比显著下降 24
4. 中国投资者偏好超短线交易，欧洲、北美时段交易量旗鼓相当 25
5. 中国投资者偏好交易现货黄金、WTI原油，其他交易标的偏好不一 26
6. 盈利账户占比 27
（二）东南亚地区 28
1. 东南亚投资者中也是男性为主，主力年龄段也为25—34岁之间 28
2. 东南亚地区投资者同样偏好超短线交易 29
3. 交易标的：新马泰投资者各不相同，越南投资者对数字货币情有独钟 30
4. 东南亚市场中IC Markets表现抢眼 30

第3部分　人民币外汇期货及人民币汇率

（一）三家主要交易所人民币期货2019年表现 32
1. 香港交易所 32
2. 新加坡交易所 34

3. 芝商所	34
（二）人民币汇率回顾与展望	37
1. 2019年人民币汇率回顾	37
2. 2020年人民币汇率展望	38
3. "一带一路"与人民币国际化	39
4. 中国外汇储备与人民币汇率	40

第4部分　全球主要交易所2019年发展情况

（一）上海黄金交易所	44
1. 2019年上海黄金交易所成交量大幅攀升	44
2. 上海黄金交易所会员金银成交量分析	48
（二）上海期货交易所	50
1. 沪金沪银价格及成交量双双暴涨	50
2. 中国原油期货交易量持续攀升	52
（三）CME旗下金银期货交易状况	54
（四）WTI及ICE布伦特原油交易状况	55
（五）交易所交易量对比	57

第5部分　东南亚市场营商环境及行业现状

前言	60
（一）经济状况	61
（二）营商环境	64
1. 劳动力市场	64
2. 外商投资	65
3. 法律环境	66

4. 经济自由度指数 66
5. 网络运营环境及互联网经济 68

（三）金融业现状 70
1. 外汇经纪行业概况 70
2. 经纪商着眼东南亚作为最新扩张目标 71
3. 积极发展金融科技 72
4. 中国金融企业进军东南亚 72
5. 保险产品在东南亚市场的状况 73

（四）中国台湾 74
1. 经济状况 74
2. 营商环境 74
3. 外汇经纪业务发展 75

第6部分　附　录

第 1 部分

全球外汇及加密货币行业热点与趋势

Foreword

With the saturation of the European and American markets in recent years, more brokers have set their sights on emerging markets, which of Southeast Asia becomes one of the most important focus. In this article, three representative Southeast Asian countries are selected for analysis, namely Vietnam, Thailand and Malaysia. Vietnam has a relatively large population of young people, with stable growth in recent years and great potential for future economic development. Economic freedom in Thailand and Malaysia ranks top amongst Southeast Asian countries. Thailand attracts overseas investment for years. Malaysia has the characteristics of successful economic transformation and higher personal income. In addition, Taiwan of China is also involved. This article analyses the performance in the industry and other related issues of this developed economy.

Part **5**

Business Environment and Industry Status in Southeast Asia

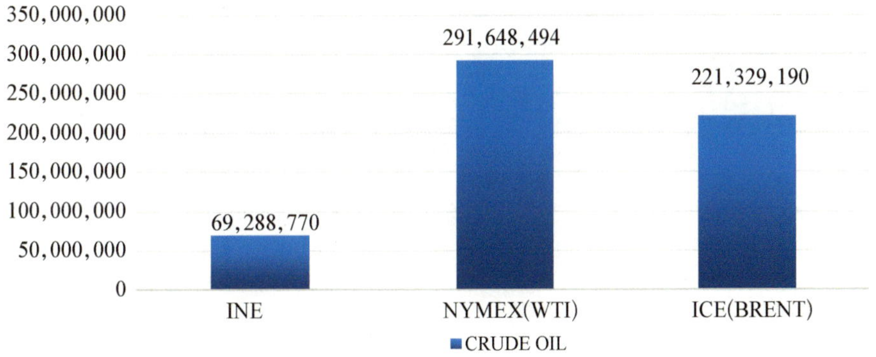

Part 4　Development of Major Global Exchanges in 2019

Figure 4-17: The Crude Oil Trading Volume of INE,NYMEX and ICE in 2019 (unit: lots)

（Ⅴ） Trading Volume Comparison between Exchanges

The following chart summarizes the comparison of the annual trading volume of the exchanges mentioned above in 2019, and the comparison targets all gold and silver contracts of the SGE, SHFE Gold Futures and Silver Futures contracts, and CME Gold and Silver Futures, INE Crude Oil Futures contracts, WTI Crude Oil Futures in CME, and Brent Crude Oil contracts in ICE.

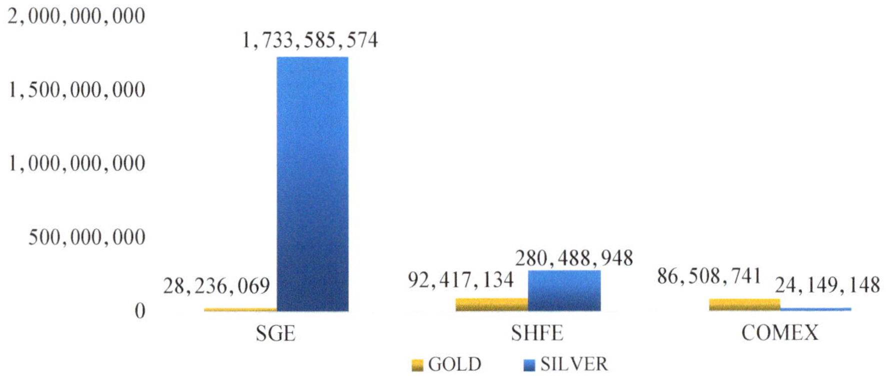

Figure 4-16: Gold and Silver Trading Volume of SGE, SHFE and COMEX in 2019 (unit: lots)

Part 4 Development of Major Global Exchanges in 2019

14,640,114 lots in December 2019 was the lowest level in 2019, and 15,863,921 lots in February was the second lowest in the year.

In contrast, the fluctuation range of WTI Crude Oil trading volume was relatively small, of which 5,370,010 lots were traded in May 2019, the highest in the year. In December 2019, the trading volume was 3,687,071, the lowest level in the year, and the trading volume in other months was volatile.

Table 4-3: ICE Brent and WTI Crude Oil Volume in 2019 (unit: lots)

Year 2019	Brent	WTI
Jan. 2019	18,333,845	4,261,645
Feb. 2019	15,863,921	3,780,835
Mar. 2019	17,581,862	4,046,162
Apr. 2019	19,056,842	4,704,316
May 2019	21,951,737	5,370,010
Jun. 2019	19,467,509	4,934,200
Jul. 2019	19,591,446	4,753,679
Aug. 2019	19,930,130	5,119,374
Sept. 2019	20,858,428	4,634,781
Oct. 2019	17,790,768	4,377,100
Nov. 2019	16,262,588	3,928,694
Dec. 2019	14,640,114	3,687,071
Total	221,329,190	53,597,867

Figure 4-15: ICE Brent and WTI Crude Oil Volume in 2019 (unit: lots)

63

（Ⅳ） WTI and ICE Brent Crude Oil

The trend of the crude oil market in 2019 was quite volatile. After consecutive sharp rises from January to April 2019, oil prices experienced a slump in May 2019, giving up most of the gains in the previous months. After a "bloodback" rally in June, crude oil prices fell into downward trend from July to October 2019 for 4 consecutive months. From November to December, it rebounded for two consecutive months. Overall, WTI Crude Oil Futures rose 2.96% throughout the year of 2019.

The total trading volume of WTI Crude Oil Futures was 291,648,494 lots in 2019, decreased 4.89% from 2018.

Table 4-2: WTI Crude Oil Futures Trading Volume in 2019(unit: lots)

Contracts	2019	2018	YoY change
CRUDE OIL PHY	291,648,494	306,637,648	↓−4.89%

According to data from Intercontinental Exchange (ICE), in 2019, the cumulative trading volume of Brent Crude Oil Futures was 221,329,190 lots, while the cumulative trading volume of WTI crude oil was 53,597,867 lots.

The monthly trading volume of Brent Crude Oil in 2019 was roughly similar to the trend WTI Crude Oil. Brent Crude recorded a highest trading volume of 21,951,737 lots in May 2019, followed by 20,858,428 lots in September 2019.

Part 4   Development of Major Global Exchanges in 2019

lots, a year-over-year increase of 269.76%.

Table 4–1: COMEX Gold and Silver Futures Trading Volume in 2019 (unit: lots)

Contracts	2019	2018	YoY change
COMEX GOLD	86,508,741	80,301,590	↑7.73%
COMEX E Mini GOLD	241,481	96,481	↑150.29%
COMEX SILVER	24,149,148	23,987,051	↑0.68%
COMEX E Mini SILVER	49,552	13,401	↑269.76%

（Ⅲ） CME Gold and Silver Futures

In 2019, the uncertainty of global trade situation continued, global geopolitical risks were rising, also with the tortuous process of Brexit, and the spread of economic recession concerns, the market sentiment was in safe-haven atmosphere, and the gold performed very well.

Affected by the uncertainty of the global environment, market sentiment fluctuated during the year, and the overall trading volume of gold was rising. As of December 2019, the total trading volume of COMEX Gold Futures was 86,508,741 lots, an increase of 7.73% year-over-year. And the trading volume of Gold Futures mini contracts showed a surging trend, with a total of 241,481 lots, a year-over-year increase of 150.29%.

The overall trend of silver was more volatile than gold. Since February 2019, it has been falling for 4 consecutive months, and it has been rising strongly for 3 consecutive months since June 2019. From September to November, it has shown a mixed trend of fluctuations. However, in terms of trading volume, COMEX Silver Futures contracts has declined comparing to the same period last year.

At the same time, as of December, the total trading volume of COMEX Silver Futures was 24,149,148 lots, a year-over-year decrease of 0.68%. In contrast, the trading volume of Silver Futures mini contracts unexpectedly soared, reached 49,552

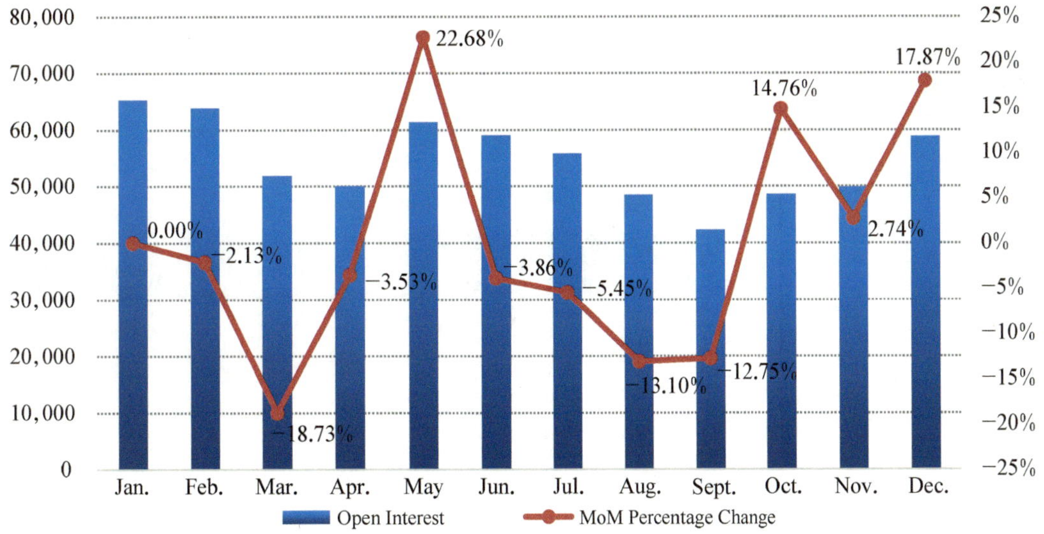

Part 4　Development of Major Global Exchanges in 2019

Figure 4-14: INE Crude Oil Futures Open Interest in 2019 (unit: lots)

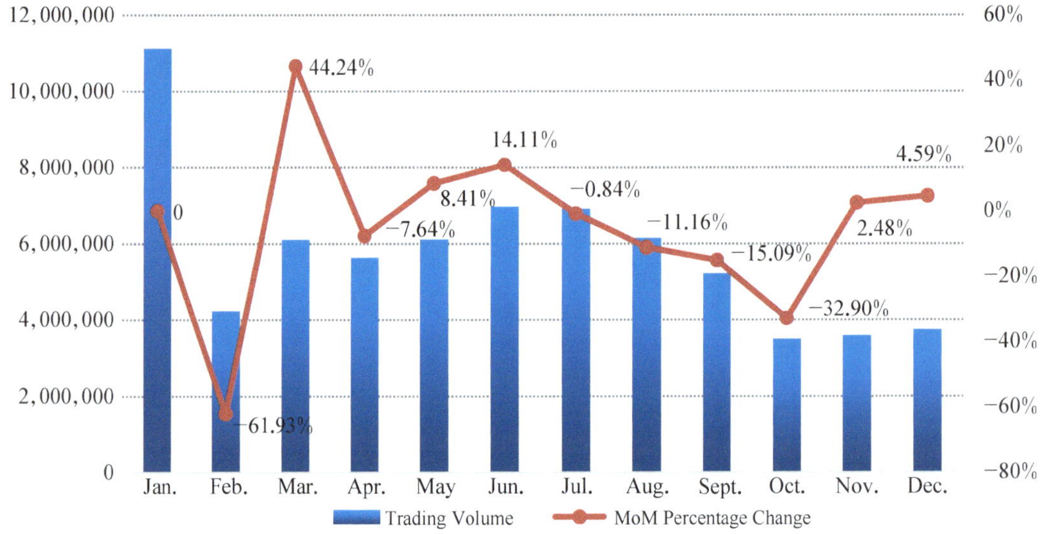

2019 Foreign Exchange and Precious Metals Market Blue Book

Figure 4–12: INE Crude Oil Futures Trading Volume 2019 (unit: lots)

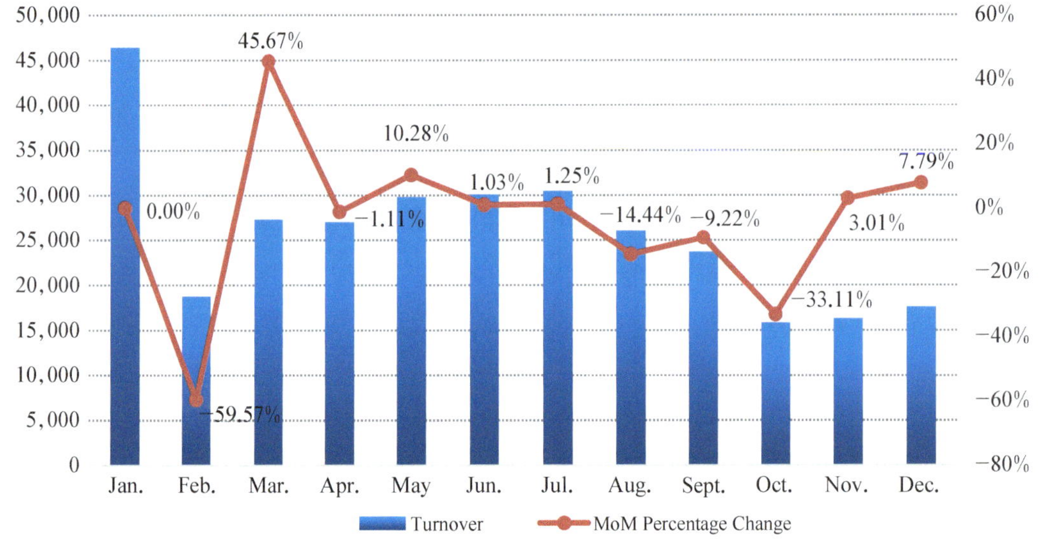

Figure 4–13: INE Crude Oil Futures Turnover in 2019 (unit: 100 million RMB)

In addition, INE Crude Oil Futures' cumulative open interest was 655,522 lots from January to December 2019. Affected by global financial market, after a significant monthly decline of 18.73% in March, the open interest gradually began to pick up, and an increase of 22.68% was recorded in May 2019. After that, open interest fell again. In August 2019, it fell 13.10% month-over-month, and then rebounded. From October to December 2019, the open interest increased for 3 consecutive months, and increased by 17.87% in December 2019.

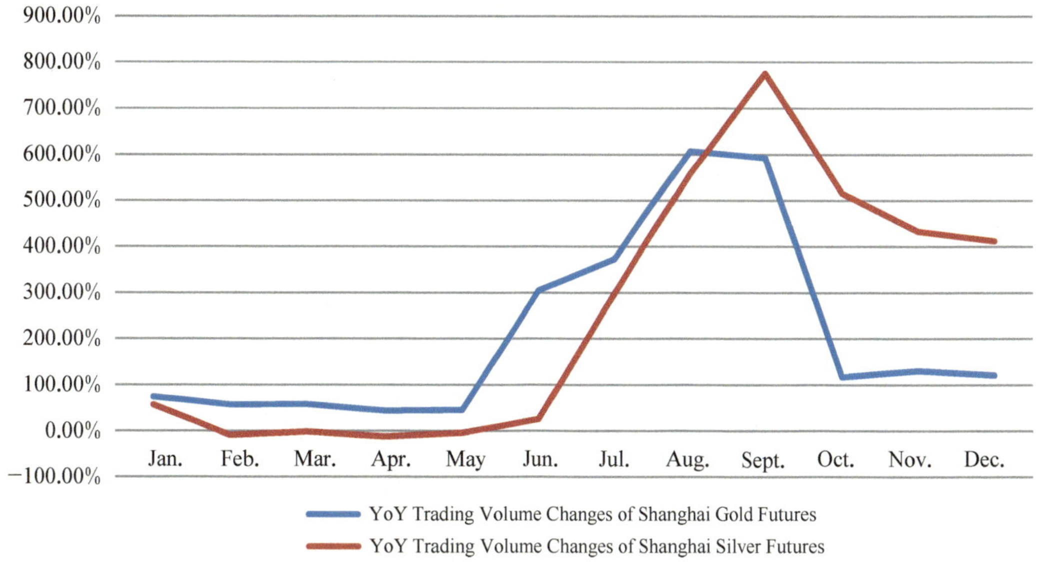

Part 4 Development of Major Global Exchanges in 2019

YoY Trading Volume Changes of Shanghai Gold Futures
YoY Trading Volume Changes of Shanghai Silver Futures

Figure 4–11: YoY Trading Volume Changes of Shanghai Gold and Silver Futures from Jan. to Dec. in 2019

derivatives and better serve the real economy.

2. China's Crude Oil Futures Trading Volume Continues to Rise

Since listing and trading in March 2018, after nearly two years of operation, China's Crude Oil Futures, traded in the Shanghai International Energy Exchange(INE), have run well and the overall trading has been active. Its trading scale has steadily ranked to the third in the world, and the open interest has also been significantly higher than the initial levels of other crude oil futures in the world.

In 2019, the cumulative trading volume of INE Crude Oil Futures was 69,288,770 lots, as 1,000 barrels per lot, it's about 69.2 billion barrels. As to the trading volume in each month, January was significantly higher than the other months in 2019, at 11,117,202 lots, and the trading volume in the following months fluctuated.

On a month-over-month basis, the trading volume in February 2019 fell sharply by 61.93%, but then rose sharply in March, achieving a 44.24% increase. In the following months, the trading volume fluctuated, and a significant decrease of 32.90% was recorded in October 2019.

At the same time, the turnover of INE Crude Oil Futures from January to December fluctuated with the trading volume in 2019, with a cumulative RMB 30,952.292 billion. In February, the turnover fell 59.57% month-on-month, and in March it rose 45.67%. In the following months, the turnover fluctuated from month to month, but a significant decrease of 33.11% was recorded in October.

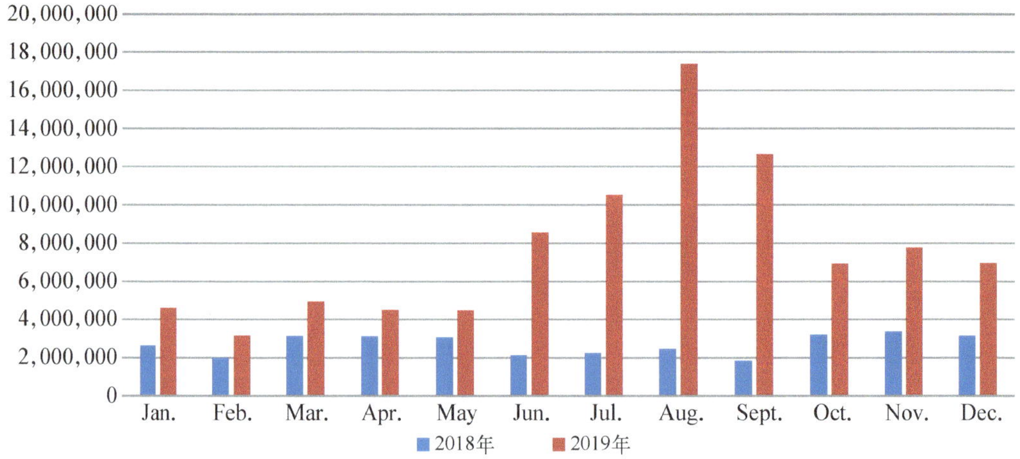

2019 Foreign Exchange and Precious Metals Market Blue Book

Figure 4-9: Monthly Trading Volume of SHFE Gold Futures in 2018 and 2019(unit: lots)

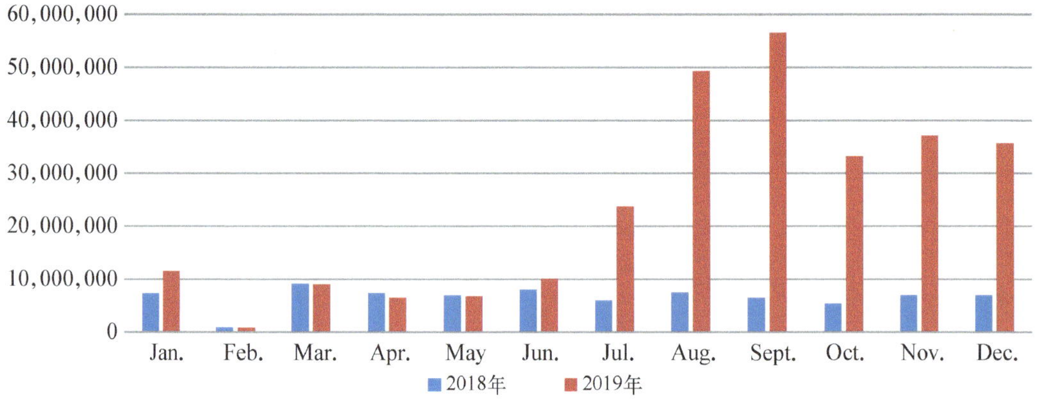

Figure 4-10: Monthly Trading Volume of SHFE Silver Futures in 2018 and 2019(unit: lots)

Futures rose sharply since May 2019, with an increase of more than 600%, and then the increase fell to about 100% in the fourth quarter. At the same time, the SHFE Silver Futures began to increase sharply since June (one month later than the gold contracts), and the increase soared to nearly 800% in September, and then fell slightly, but increase in the fourth quarter still exceeded 400%, which was obvious higher than SHFE Gold Futures.

It is worth mentioning that, as an important part of the China gold market, SHFE Gold Futures have been in operation for 11 years. Since its listing, the overall operation has been stable, the trading scale has increased steadily, physical delivery has been orderly, and the prices are highly correlated with international gold prices. In order to compliment the existing trading strategies and improve the risk management capabilities of commercial banks, SHFE launched the first precious metal option on December 20, 2019-SHFE Gold Options were officially listed for trading. Wang Fenghai, General Manager of SHFE, said the listing of Gold Options could further enrich the gold

(II) Shanghai Futures Exchange

1. Shanghai Gold and Silver Futures Prices and Trading Volume Both Skyrocketed

The global trade conflict in 2019 caused recession concerns and the Federal Reserve cut interest rates three times, which stimulated demand for safe havens. Spot gold price had skyrocketed since the end of May 2019, reaching a six-year high of around $ 1,557/ounce in early September. At the same time, spot silver also hit a three-year high of $19.65/ounce in September. Corresponding to this, the gold and silver futures prices traded in Shanghai Futures Exchanges (SHFE) and the trading volume both grew on a large scale.

For the trading volume of SHFE in 2019, Shanghai Gold Futures and Silver Futures both surged year-over-year. For Gold Futures, the trading volume surged significantly 186.58% compared with 2018, and Silver Futures recorded an increase of 254.14%.

Data showed that, the total trading volume of SHFE Gold Futures in 2019 was 92,417,134 lots, as 1,000 grams per lot; the volume was 92,417,134,000 grams, or 92,417.13 tons, a surge of over 180% year-on-year. At the same time, the trading volume of SHFE Silver Futures totaled 280,488,948 lots, as 15 kg per lot; the trading volume was 4,207,334,220 kg, which was 4,207,334.22 tons, a surge of over 250% year-on-year.

On year-over-year base, trading volume of SHFE Gold

but its share has gone from close to 13% to less than 10%, and it dropped out of the top list in the following 7 months. SPD Bank did not enter into the list in June, but for the other 11 months it made to the list, and its trading volume was steady to rising pattern. From January to May, it ranked NO.3 and then rose to be NO.2 in July, October, November, and December.

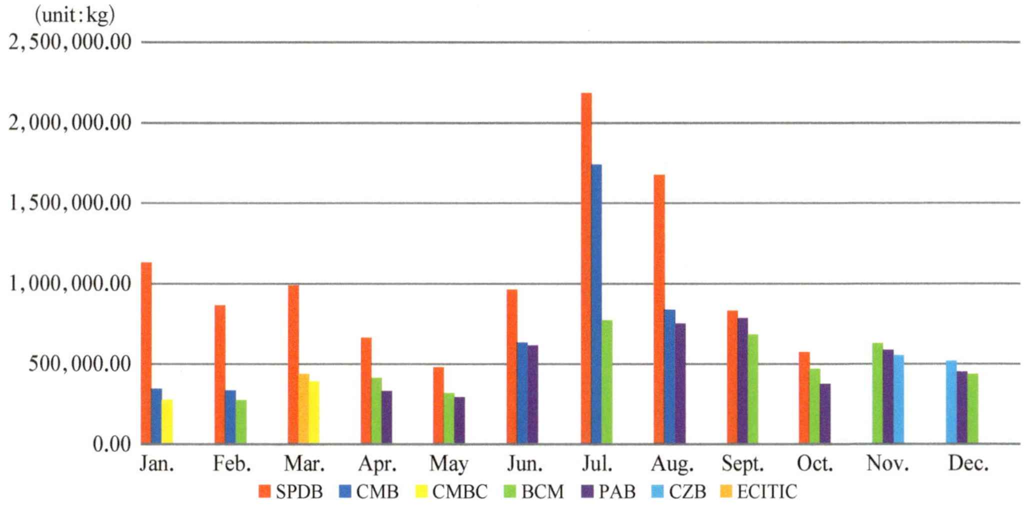

Part 4　Development of Major Global Exchanges in 2019

(unit：kg)

Figure 4-7: Top Three Position in Monthly Gold Trading Volume among SGE Members in 2019

As for silver, ICBC and Jump Trading were the most frequent traders in 2019. The data showed that in 2019, ICBC appeared in top three every month, and kept being NO.1 for 7 consecutive months since the beginning of the year, but the proportion of trading volume in the next 5 months gradually decreased. From August to September, ICBC was the second place, and from October to December, it ranked to be the third place.

Quantitative trading agency Jump Trading was the latecomer. Since June 2019 it jumped to Top 3 in trading volume, and continued to be the NO.1 since August. In terms of total trading volume, it was far ahead, the trading volume in the single month of September accounted for 20.34%.

Ping An Bank and SPD Bank also were the frequent visitors of Top 3 in terms of trading volume. Since the beginning of 2019, Ping An Bank ranked second for 5 consecutive months,

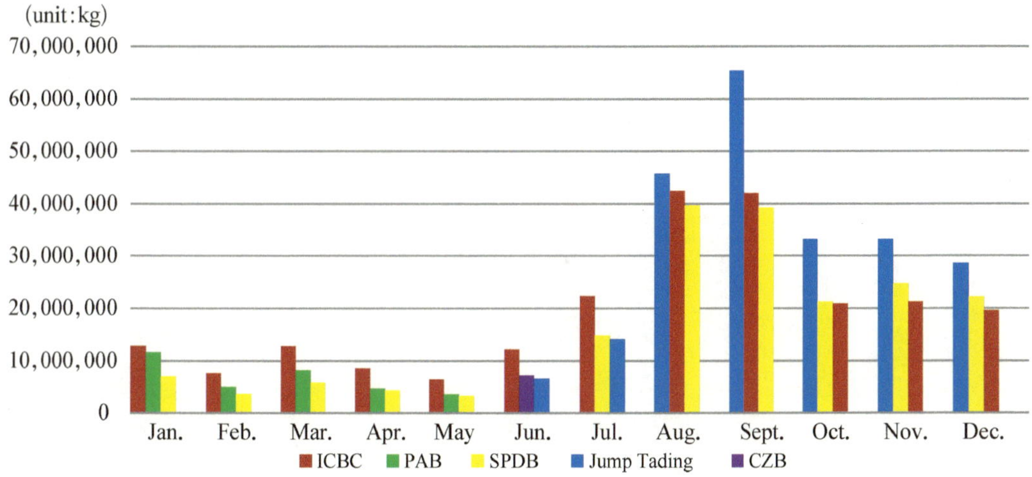

(unit：kg)

Figure 4-8: Top3 Members in Terms of Monthly Silver Trading Volume in 2019

53

2019 Foreign Exchange and Precious Metals Market Blue Book

approached the 1,000,000 kg. The month-over-month increase from more than 60% to stable, and the month-on-month increase was about 30% in December.

From the perspective of price trends, the benchmark price of SHAG has been fluctuating at a high level since its introduction in October 2019, and then sharply declined and consolidated in November. It once approached 4,025 RMB/kg, and rose again strongly in December 2019, returning back to the high level of 4,350 RMB/kg at the end of October 2019.

Figure 4–6: Monthly Price of SHAG in 2019 (RMB/kg)

Source: Shanghai Gold Exchange.

2. Analysis of Gold and Silver Trading Volume of SGE Members

According to the SGE, Shanghai Pudong Development Bank(SPD Bank), Ping An Bank, and Bank of Communications(BCM) were the most active members in gold trading in 2019. In the 12 months of 2019, SPD Bank consecutively topped in monthly gold trading volume from January to October. The trading volume in January, February and July all accounted for more than 20%, and the monthly trading volume showed a pattern similar to "И".

Unlike the SPD Bank's continuous leading, Ping An Bank kept in the top three in 8 of the 12 months in 2019, consistently ranked second or third in the second quarter to the fourth quarter (except July). The highest trading volume proportion was 12.91% in September. BCM also entered into the top three for eight times in the 12 months of 2019, and listed to be NO.1 in November, with the trading volume accounted for 12.15%. In the remaining seven months, BCM recorded the second for 3 times and the third for 4 times.

In addition, China Merchants Bank(CMB) and Minsheng Bank(CMBC) also often ranked among top three in the gold trading volume among SGE members. In 2019, CMB ranked second for 5 months, and the trading volume reached the highest in July, accounting for 17.59%. CMBC ranked among the top three twice.

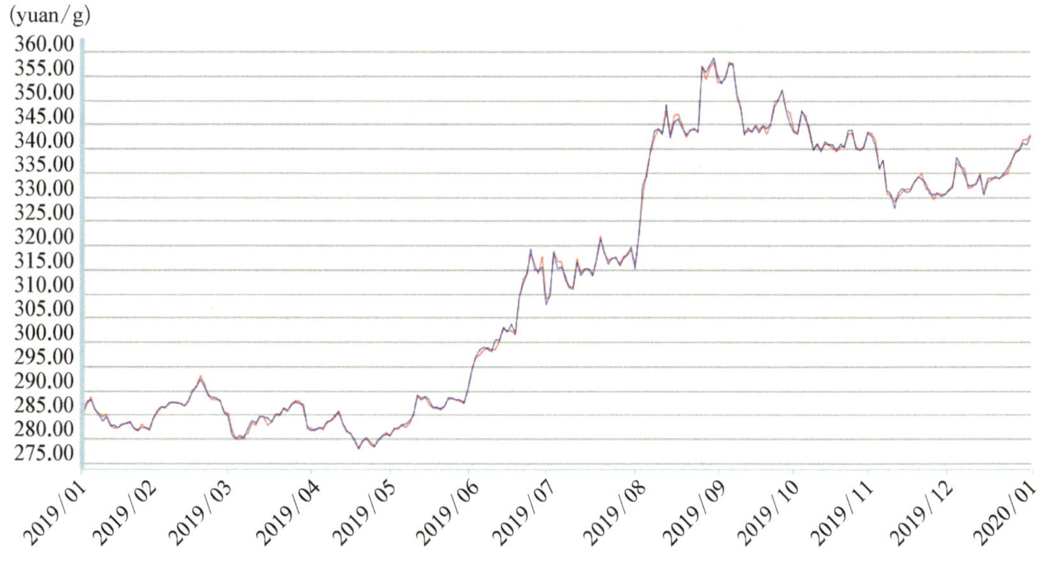

Part 4   Development of Major Global Exchanges in 2019

(yuan/g)

Figure 4-4: Monthly Price of SHAU in 2019

Source: Shanghai Gold Exchange.

In terms of silver contracts, according to data, the total trading volume of silver contracts including Ag (T+D), Ag99.99 and Shanghai Silver SHAG in 2019 totaled 1,733,585,574.00 kg, or approximately 1,733,585.57 Tons, a significant increase from 2018. Among them, the cumulative trading volume of Ag (T+D) contracts in 2019 soared by 120.89% year-over-year, and the trading volume of Ag99.99 contracts dropped by 38.55% year-over-year.

It was also worth mentioning that the Shanghai Silver SHAG started centralized pricing trial operation on September 16, 2019, and officially listed on October 14, 2019, quickly gained its place in the market. The trading volume of SHAG within 2.5 months exceeded the trading volume of Ag99.99 in the whole year of 2019, accounted for about 0.14% of the total trading volume of the silver contracts. From September to December 2019, the monthly trading volume of SHAG contract gradually climbed. In December, the trading volume

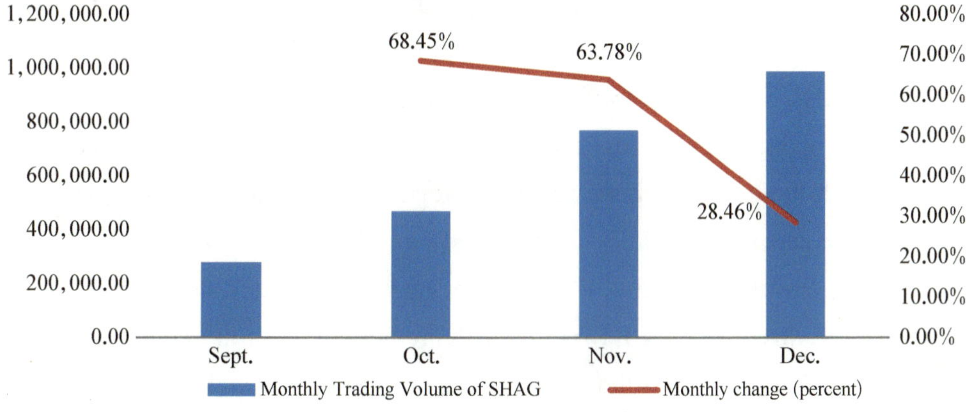

Figure 4-5: Monthly Trading Volume of SHAG(unit: kg)

to data from the Shanghai Gold Exchange, the cumulative trading volume of Shanghai Gold SHAU from January to December 2019 was 1,168,964.00 kg, or approximately 1,168.96 tons, a significant drop of 20.73% comparing to the same period in 2018.

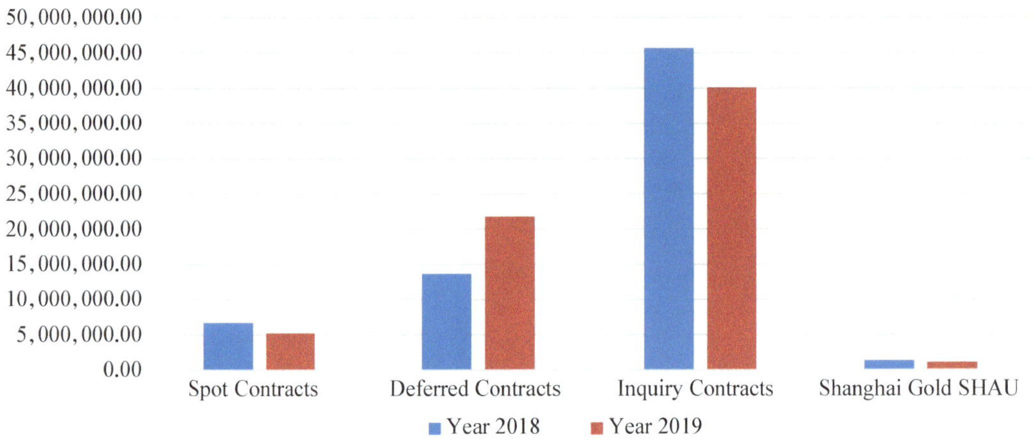

Figure 4-2: Contracts Trading Volume of SGE in 2018 and 2019 (unit: kg)

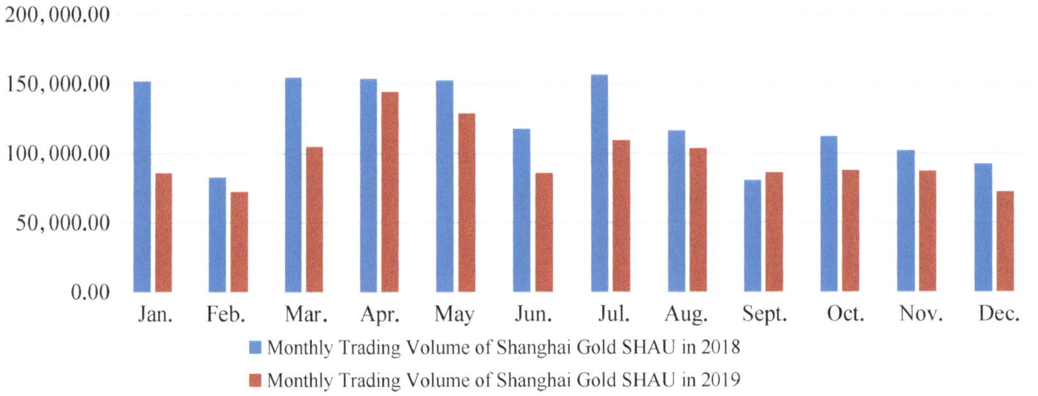

Figure 4-3: Monthly Trading Volume of SHAU in 2018 and 2019 (unit: kg)

From the perspective of monthly trading volume yearly change, SHAU's trading volume declined in 11 months and only rose in September, the increase was 7.07%. At the beginning of September, spot gold once reached above $1,550 per ounce, and the benchmark price of SHAU reached above the highest level of 355 yuan/gram at the end of August. In other months, the year-over-year declines in January, March and July were the highest, reaching 43.61%, 32.23% and 29.99% respectively.

From the perspective of the volume proportion, the status of inquiry contracts was still solid. The data showed that the trading volume of the inquiry contracts in 2019 accounted for 58.77% of the total trading volume of the Shanghai Gold Exchange. At the same time, the trading volume of deferred contracts in 2019 accounted for more than 30%, while spot contracts continued to fall to less than 10%, and SHAU contracts accounted for less than 2%.

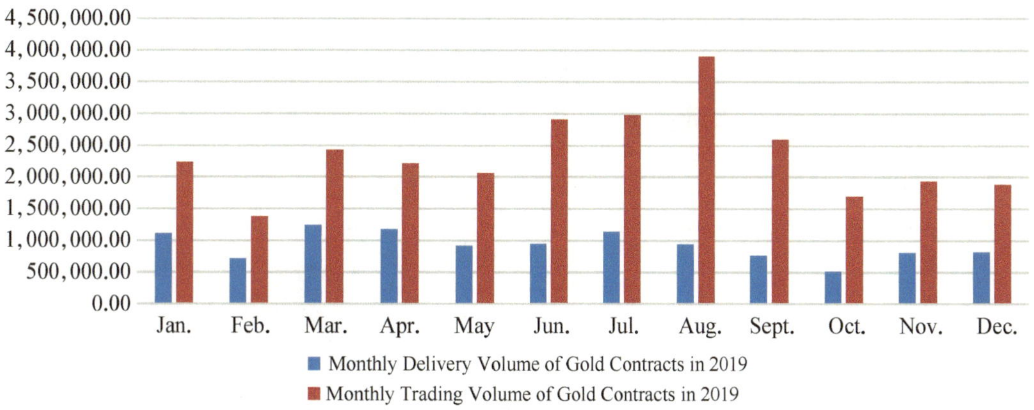

Part 4 Development of Major Global Exchanges in 2019

Figure 4-1: Gold Trading Volume and Delivery Volume of SGE in 2019 (unit: kg)

to 11,104.56 tons, a slight decrease of 4.72% compared with the same period in 2018.

In terms of spot contracts, the cumulative trading volume of contracts including Au99.99, Au99.95, Au100g and iAu9999 from January to December 2019 was 5,214,024.78 kg, or approximately 5,214.02 tons, a significant decrease of 22.56% comparing to the same period in 2018. Among them, the trading volume of the Au99.95 contract fell the most on a yearly basis, reaching 40.08%. While the trading volume of the Au99.99 contract was the second largest decrease, reaching 23.59%. The decrease of iAu9999 was the smallest, only 3.40%. Meanwhile, the volume of Au100g contract rose 19.30% year-over-year, which was the best performing one in all spot contracts.

For deferred contracts, from January to December 2019, the cumulative trading volume of Au (T+D), mAu (T+D), Au (T+N1), and Au (T+N2) contracts was 21,814,912.00 kg, or about 21,814.91 tons, surged by nearly 60% compared with 2018. Among them, the mAu (T+D) contract volume increased the most year-over-year, reaching a staggering 119.55%. As the most actively traded contract, the cumulative trading volume of the Au (T+D) contract over the 12-month period increased significantly by 60.33% year-over-year. The cumulative trading volume of the Au(T+N1) and Au(T+N2) contracts declined 35.45% and 32.46% respectively.

In terms of the inquiry contracts, from January to December 2019, the cumulative trading volume including inquiry Au99.95, inquiry Au99.99, inquiry OAu99.99, and inquiry iAu99.99 contracts was 40,086,274.56 kg, about 40,086.27 tons, a slight decrease of 12.18% comparing to the same period in 2018. Among them, the trading volume of the Au99.99 inquiry contract declined the most on the yearly basis, reaching 17.34%, and the trading volume of the Au99.95 inquiry contract recorded the second largest decrease of 8.50%. But, the trading volume of iAu99.99 contract unexpectedly increased 6.77% comparing to 2018.

China's gold fixing price—"Shanghai Gold" trading volume fell significantly. According

（Ⅰ） Shanghai Gold Exchange

1. Shanghai Gold Exchange's Trading Volume Soars in 2019

Risk aversion was a theme that could not be ignored in the global market in 2019. International gold prices had risen sharply from June to September, which was also reflected in different gold contracts of Shanghai Gold Exchange (SGE). From January to December 2019, trading volume of various gold contracts of the Shanghai Gold Exchange increased significantly comparing to the same period of 2018. Among them, the trading volume from June to September exceeded 2.5 million kilograms, but the gold contracts delivery volume declined slightly year-on-year.

The data from SGE showed that the cumulative delivery volume of gold contracts in 2019 decreased slightly year-over-year, while the cumulative trading volume of gold contracts increased significantly compared with the same period in 2018. Among them, trading volume of deferred contracts increased rapidly overall, inquiry contracts fell slightly, while trading volume of spot contracts fell sharply year-on-year.

Data as of December 31, 2019 showed that, In January-December 2019, a total of 28,236,069.20 kilograms of gold contracts were traded, equivalent to 28,236.07 tons, a near 30% increase from the same period in 2018. At the same time, SGE delivered a total of 11,104,563.00 kilograms of gold, equivalent

Part **4**

Development of Major Global Exchanges in 2019

period of RMB appreciation in 2017, foreign exchange reserves increased; during the period of RMB depreciation in 2018, foreign exchange reserves decreased.

However, it is worth noting that from April to August 2019, RMB continued to depreciate due to the appreciation of the US dollar, but its foreign exchange reserves have remained relatively stable. The RMB fell below 7.0000 in August, but the size of China's foreign exchange reserves continued to rise during that month.

Why does this happen? The reasons may be as follows: First, the demand for residents' purchase of foreign exchange has not increased significantly. Secondly, domestic and overseas residents and enterprises have not experienced capital outflows.

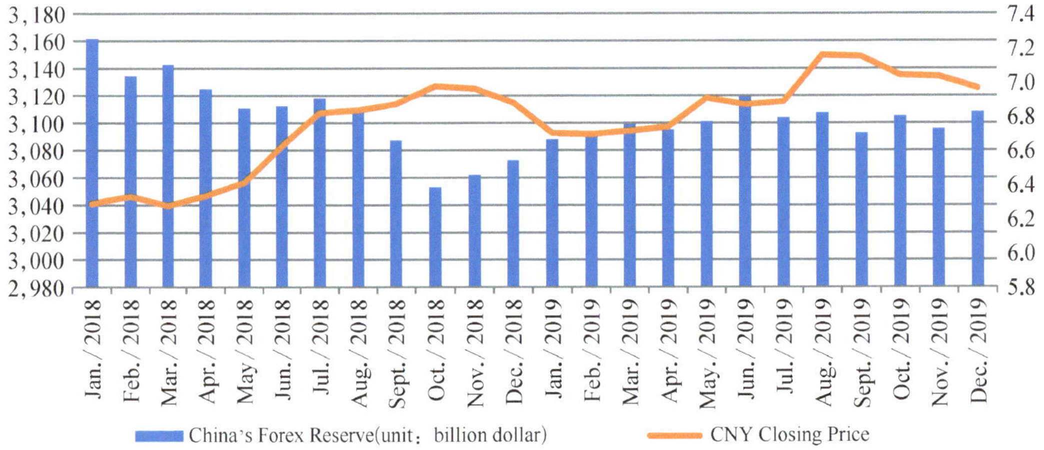

Figure 3-8: China's Forex Reserve VS. CNY Closing Price

Market analysis believed that the size of China's foreign exchange reserves may further increase in 2020. However, due to the outbreak of the coronavirus, the International Monetary Fund has lowered its forecast for China's economic growth in 2020. The continuation of the coronavirus will definitely have an impact on the size of China's foreign exchange reserves.

Monetary Fund (IMF), the proportion of RMB in foreign reserves rose to 2.01% in the third quarter of 2019. This is the highest level since the fourth quarter of 2016 that the IMF began to report the proportion of RMB assets held by central banks in various economies.

In October 2016, the RMB was officially added to the SDR currency basket, marking RMB an official major international reserve currency. Since then, the proportion of RMB in global external reserves has been on the rise. At present, more than 60 foreign central banks or monetary authorities have incorporated the RMB into their foreign exchange reserves.

The report issued by SWIFT pointed out that the "Belt and Road" initiative provides major opportunities for Chinese and foreign banks doing business in countries along the route, and has become a promoter of RMB internationalization.

Dong Liu, Director and Associate Professor of the World Economic Research Institute, said on November 23, 2019 that the "Belt and Road" provides new opportunities for RMB internationalization. He believes that the construction of the "Belt and Road" and the internationalization of the RMB are mutual promotion and coordinated development. From the perspective of cross-border trade, infrastructure construction, and financial platforms, the "Belt and Road" has a positive effect on promoting the internationalization of the RMB.

Liu Dong pointed out that for the RMB, trade, investment and financial platforms are the three main paths of the "Belt and Road" to promote RMB internationalization.

Cao Yuanzheng, Chairman of BOC International Research Corporation, said on June 8, 2019 that the use of RMB in the "Belt and Road" will increase. As a major trade currency, investment currency and financing currency, RMB's functions continue to be used.

In fact, the "Belt and Road" and RMB internationalization are complementary. Pan Gongsheng, deputy governor of the People's Bank of China, wrote in July 2019 that judging from the practice in recent years, the gradual expansion of the international use of RMB has played an increasingly important role in implementing the "Belt and Road" initiative.

Of course, the implementation of the "Belt and Road" initiative has been questioned in varying degrees, including China's motivations for lending to countries along the "Belt and Road", the ability of countries to repay their loans, and the sustainability of Chinese lending.

4. China's Foreign Exchange Reserves VS. RMB Exchange Rate

Judging from the trend of RMB exchange rate and foreign exchange reserves in the past few years, the two generally show a positive correlation. The logic behind this trend is that during the period of RMB appreciation, the central bank intentionally bought more US dollars to stabilize the exchange rate. During the period of RMB depreciation, the central bank will sell foreign exchange, and foreign exchange reserves will decrease. For example, during the

Institutions	USD/RMB Expectation	Expectation Notes	Release Time
Ping An	6.9–7.4	The epidemic affects the RMB exchange rate mainly through the following two channels in short-term: first, the epidemic will reduce the risk appetite of market entities; second, the spread between China and US is expected to narrow. The RMB exchange rate may face some depreciation pressure in 2020, but the amplitude is controllable.	January 2020
Morgan Stanley	6.85	Raise expectation of RMB vs US dollar rate.	December 2019
Commerzbank	7.23	Given the slowdown in economic growth and trade uncertainty, the RMB is expected to depreciate mildly in the coming years.	December 2019
Shenwan	6.8	RMB exchange rate is expected to rise further.	December 2019
Monita	N/A	The attractiveness of RMB assets has increased, and RMB assets are expected to gradually be favored by global asset allocation agencies.	December 2019

3. The "Belt and Road" and RMB Internationalization

The "Belt and Road" is the abbreviation of "Silk Road Economic Belt" and "21st Century Maritime Silk Road". In September and October 2013, President Xi Jinping proposed cooperation initiatives to build the "New Silk Road Economic Belt" and the "21st Century Maritime Silk Road". With the advancement of the "Belt and Road" initiative, RMB internationalization developed rapidly in recent years.

The proposal of the "Belt and Road" initiative has deepened the regional trade and investment and financing cooperation between China and neighboring countries, continuously expand the RMB-denominated financial market, and hastened the process of RMB internationalization. The "Belt and Road" construction requires huge amounts of capital, and huge capital needs require long-term and stable capital investment, which is conducive to the export of RMB under capital accounts. By adopting the RMB for cross-border trade valuation and settlement, the countries along the "Belt and Road" can effectively avoid the risk of large fluctuations in international exchange rates, reduce exchange costs, and promote the development of import and export in the region.

For six years since the Belt and Road Initiative's launch, RMB has gradually developed into one of the major international currencies. According to data released by the International

the RMB exchange rate to stabilize and recover; the RMB exchange rate was expected to improve due to the stability of economic fundamentals and other factors; the Sino-US trade war showed signs of easing.

2. Outlook of RMB in 2020

Looking forward to 2020, the movement of US dollar, China's economic fundamentals and the trade situation will still affect the trend of the RMB. In view of the downward pressure on the Chinese economy (especially the downward pressure on the economy caused by the outbreak of new coronavirus from late 2019 to early 2020), and external uncertainties remain large, the RMB exchange rate may still fluctuate in 2020. However, the impact of the epidemic on the RMB is expected to be temporary. As the epidemic ferments and its impact on the economy further manifests, the RMB exchange rate will be under pressure in a certain stage. However, as the epidemic subsides, the RMB exchange rate will return to a two-way movement.

From the official perspective, there will be no major fluctuations in the RMB exchange rate. Yi Gang, President of the People's Bank of China, stated on December 1, 2019 that the RMB exchange rate is determined by market supply and demand, and China will not instrument the exchange rate or engage in competitive devaluation. In the next stage, the People's Bank of China will continue to promote the reform of the RMB exchange rate marketization mechanism, maintain exchange rate flexibility, and will implement the necessary macro-prudential management when the market shows signs of pro-cyclicality, and keep the RMB exchange rate stable at a reasonable and balanced level.

At the end of 2019, some investment banks and institutions believed that the RMB exchange rate is expected to stabilize and recover in 2020. Due to the evolution of the epidemic in early 2020, various institutions have also given their views on the possible pressure on the RMB exchange rate.

Table 3-3: Expectations and Prospects of RMB Exchange Rate in 2020

Institutions	USD/RMB Expectation	Expectation Notes	Release Time
UBS	7.0	The economic slowdown caused by the epidemic has put pressure on the RMB, but China promises to keep the RMB exchange rate stable and the current account surplus expected to improve should provide some support for the RMB.	January 2020

(continued)

2019 Foreign Exchange and Precious Metals Market Blue Book

USD/CNY, Daily   O: 6.9280   H: 6.9383   L: 6.9203   C: 6.9215

Figure 3–7: USD/CHY Daily Chart

Source: FX168.

signs of further rising trade tensions have boosted the demand for safe-haven dollars, of which US President Trump was the most critical role, including increasing tariffs on the EU, impasse in Sino-US trade negotiations, and threatening to impose tariffs on Japan, all made the market risk aversion higher.

The second stage: early May 2019 to late July 2019. During this period, the RMB depreciated against the US dollar by about 2.2%, effectively returning to the level at the beginning of the year.

The third stage: early August 2019 to the end of August 2019. The cumulative depreciation of RMB against the US dollar during this period reached 3.7%, and it broke "7" on August 5,2019. It was worth noting that from the beginning of May to the end of August, the appreciation of the US dollar index was only about 1.4%, which indicated that the depreciation of the RMB was partly due to the strengthening of the US dollar, but also affected by other factors, including the trade war and China listed as a "currency manipulator" by the United States.

The fourth stage: early September 2019 to the end of 2019. The RMB strengthened against the US dollar during this period, accumulating a cumulative appreciation of about 2.6%, and "back to 6" on November 5, 2019. During this period, the US dollar index fell and its depreciation rate was about 0.6%. Other factors driving the appreciation of the RMB included: the overall stability of China's economic fundamentals has laid the foundation for

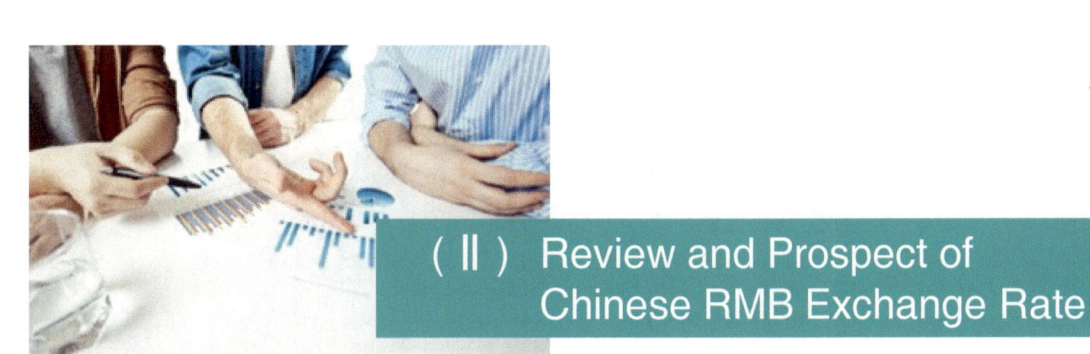

(II) Review and Prospect of Chinese RMB Exchange Rate

1. Review of RMB in 2019

Since 2019, Chinese RMB has shown a trend of declining against the US dollar, with a depreciation rate of more than 2%. On August 5, 2019, US Dollar against CHY and CNH both broke through 7. The strengthening of the US dollar index was the main factor for the decline of the RMB, however, the trade war was also another important reason for the weakening of the RMB.

As of December 31, 2019, the onshore RMB against the US dollar closed at 6.9662, and depreciated by about 1.4% in the year.

Since the beginning of 2019, the development of RMB exchange rate can be divided into the following stages:

The first stage: beginning of the year to the end of April, 2019. During this period, the RMB has generally appreciated against the US dollar, with an appreciation rate of about 2.1%. During this period, the US dollar index rose by about 1.5%, which indicated that the strengthening of the RMB was mainly due to the strengthening of its intrinsic value. An important factor in the strength of the US dollar was the relatively strong performance of the US economy. Compared with other major economies such as the Eurozone and Japan, the US economy has shown a relatively good situation in early 2019.

Another key factor is hedging in the market. In particular,

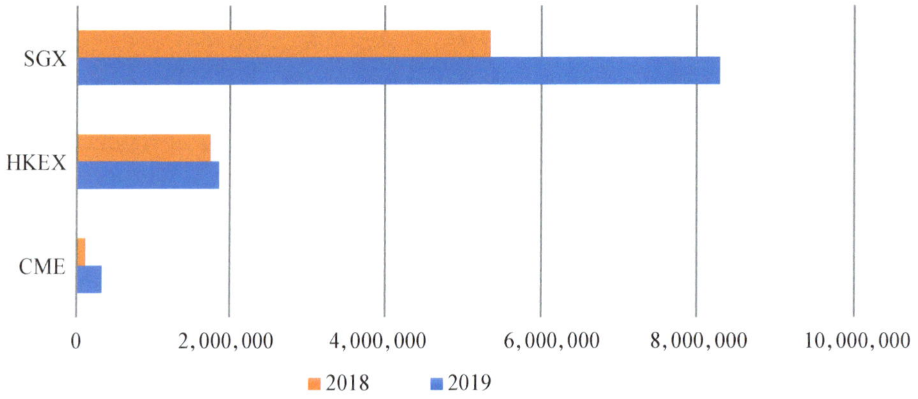

2019 Foreign Exchange and Precious Metals Market Blue Book

Figure 3–6: SGX, HKEX and CME CNH Futures Trading Volume in 2018&2019 (unit: lots)

among all 49 FX Futures on the exchange.

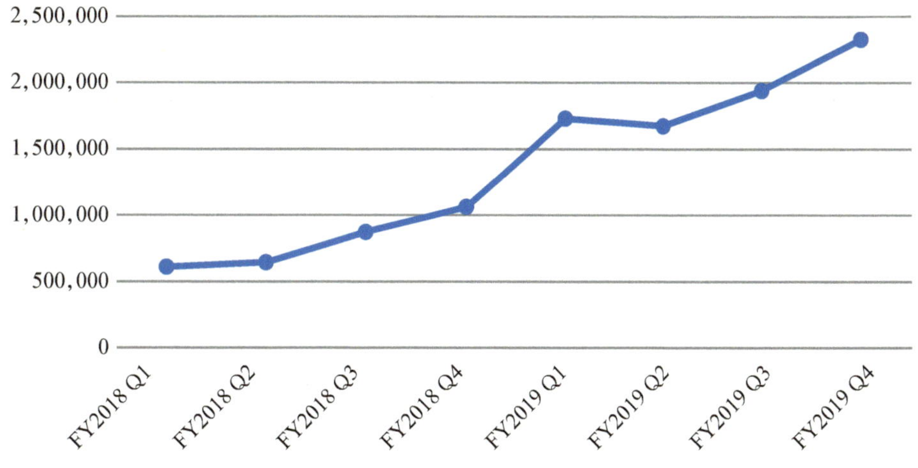

Part 3 RMB Futures and RMB Exchange Rate

Figure 3–4: USD/CNH Futures Quarterly Trading Volume of SGX (unit: lots)

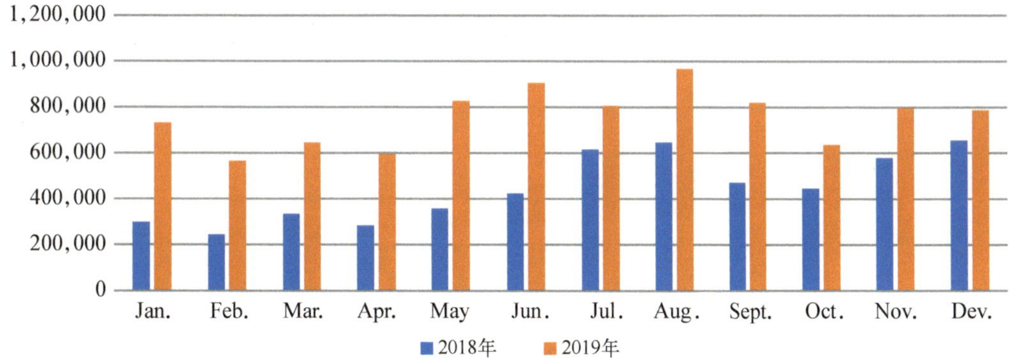

Figure 3–5: SGX RMB Futures Monthly Trading Volume in 2018&2019 (unit: lots)

The highest trading volume was also in August 2019, with 966,856 contracts. This was followed by June, when trading volume reached 904,847 contracts. This was also the only month during the year when the trading volume exceeds 900,000 contracts. The lowest trading volume was in February 2019, with 566,037 contracts.

3. CNH Futures of CME

As the world's largest foreign exchange futures exchange, CNH Futures of CME also performed well in 2019, with a total of 329,142 contracts. But this was obviously lower than the performance of HKEX and SGX.

However, CNY Futures of CME performed much year over year. The CNH trading volume during the same period of 2018 was 117,420 contracts, which meant that the year-on-year growth rate in 2019 was as high as 180.30%.

In 2019, the average daily trading volume of CME CNH Futures was 1,306 contracts, an increase of 180.3% compared to 466 contracts in 2018, one of the highest annual growth rate

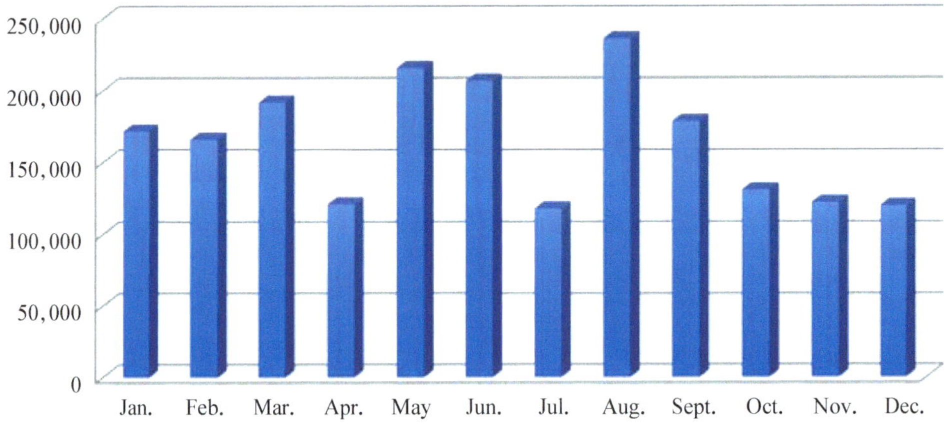

2019 Foreign Exchange and Precious Metals Market Blue Book

Figure 3-3: HKEX CNH Futures Monthly Trading Volume in 2019 (Contracts)

volume occurred on August 5, 2019, when the trading volume reached 24,345 contracts. The highest trading volume of YEN/CNH and AUD/CNH futures occurred on May 7, 2019, with a daily trading volume of 192 and 387 contracts, respectively. The highest trading volume of CNH/USD futures occurred on February 4, 2019, with a trading volume of 523 contracts on that day.

Table 3-2: The Highest Trading Volume of Five CNH Futures Products

Record High	Trading Volume	Date	Open Interest	Date	Initial Launch
USD/CNH	24,345	2019-08-05	46,711	2017-01-04	2012-09-17
EUR/CNH	431	2018-08-16	1,038	2018-09-06	2016-05-30
JPY/CNH	192	2019-05-07	491	2018-09-10	2016-05-30
AUD/CNH	387	2019-05-07	243	2019-06-17	2016-05-30
CNH/USD	523	2019-02-04	1,703	2017-01-12	2016-05-30

2. CNH Futures of SGX

The increase rate of CNH futures trading volume on the Singapore Exchange in 2019 was quite impressive, especially in November, USD/CNH trading volume reached 796,315 contracts, more than doubling the same period in 2018. Such future were also the main product of CNH futures on the exchange. Looking at the wider quarterly performance, the trading volume continued to rise.

The SGX also offers three other RMB futures products, including CHY(Online Renminbi)/USD, EUR/CNH and SGD/CNH. The monthly performance of all RMB futures in 2019 were as figure 3-5, comparing with 2018.

38

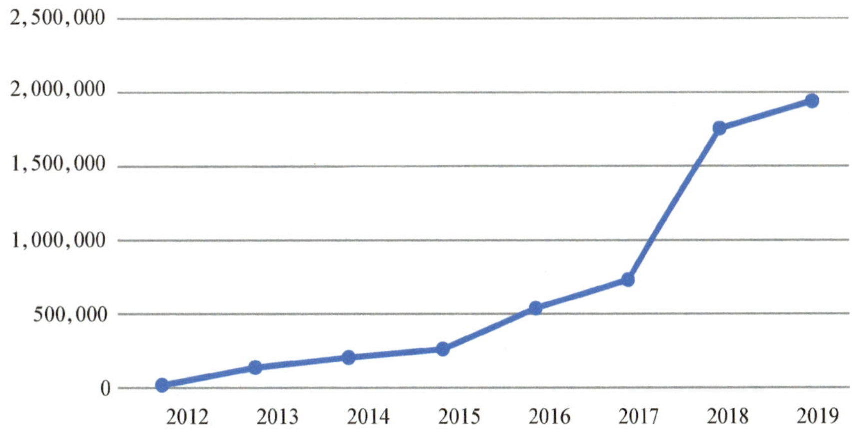

Part 3　RMB Futures and RMB Exchange Rate

Figure 3–1: USD/CNH Futures Annual Trading Volume of HKEX (unit: lots)

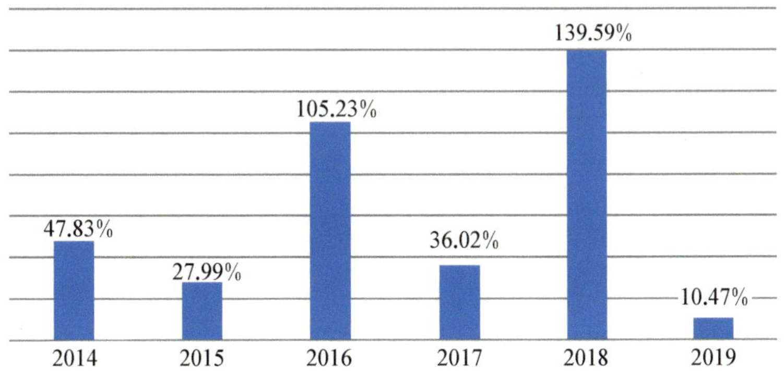

Figure 3–2: HKEX USD/CNH Futures Annual Trading Increase Rate(y/y)

2012, and the other four were issued in May 2016. In 2019, the USD/CNH trading volume accounted for 97.99% of all CNH Futures turnover. Although still an absolute majority, it has decreased comparing with 99% in 2018.

Table 3–1: CNH Futures Proportion of HKEX (2019)

Products	USD/CNH	EUR/CNH	JPY/CNH	AUD/CNH	CNH/USD
Trading Volume	1,938,891	14,656	4,689	8,277	11,759
Proportion	98.01%	0.74%	0.24%	0.42%	0.59%

Looking at the monthly performance of the trading volume of all CNH futures, the most active month was in August 2019, with a total of 236,023 contracts. The second highest month was in May 2019 with a trading volume of 215,547 contracts. In 2019, only these two months exceeded 200,000 contracts. The lowest month was in July 2019, with 117,769 contracts.

From the record of the highest trading volume of five CNH futures products, with the exception of EUR/CNH, the other four all occurred in 2019. The highest USD/CNH trading

（Ⅰ） Performance of RMB Futures on Three Major Exchanges in 2019

In 2019, the performance of CNH (Offshore Renminbi) futures have attracted the attention of many investors. On the one hand, the world's attention to China and even the CNH has increased with China's role in the world; on the other hand, market fluctuations caused by many risk events that affect investors, such as the Sino-US trade dispute, have also brought more trading opportunities, and the need to hedge investment risk in the form of derivatives such as futures. Under such circumstances, the trading volume of CNH futures on the Hong Kong Exchanges and Clearing Limited(HKEX), Singapore Exchange(SGX) and Chicago Mercantile Exchange(CME) also showed varying degrees of performance.

1. CNH Futures of HKEX

As the global offshore RMB trading center, the trading volume of the USD/CNH on the HKEX remains stable in 2019. Compared to 1,755,130 contracts in 2018, a total of 1,938,891 contracts in 2019 also means an increase of 10.5%.

It can be seen that since 2012, the trading volume of the USD/CNH Futures of HKEX has kept increasing every year. But the increase in 2019 was the lowest in the past six years.

HKEX currently offers five CNH Futures products, including USD/CNH, EUR/CNH, JPY/CNH, AUD/CNH, and CNH/USD. USD/CNH Futures began to be issued in September

Part **3**

RMB Futures and RMB Exchange Rate

Part 2　Retail Investor Structure and Behavior in Forex Markets in China and Southeast Asia

3. Transaction Subject: Investors are Different in Singapore and Malaysia and Thailand; Vietnamese Investors Prefer Digital Currencies

TradingView data shows that Southeast Asian investors generally prefer forex trading in 2019, but also prefer cryptocurrencies over Chinese investors. Especially for Vietnamese investors, their digital currency transactions account for 42.25% which is the same proportion with forex trading. From the data, Singapore, Malaysia and Thailand investors have different preferences. Singapore investors prefer forex, Malaysia investors prefer stocks, and Thailand is relatively average. Instead, the trading preferences of Indonesian and Singapore investors are more similar. For example, the forex trading of investors in these two countries both account for more than 70%.

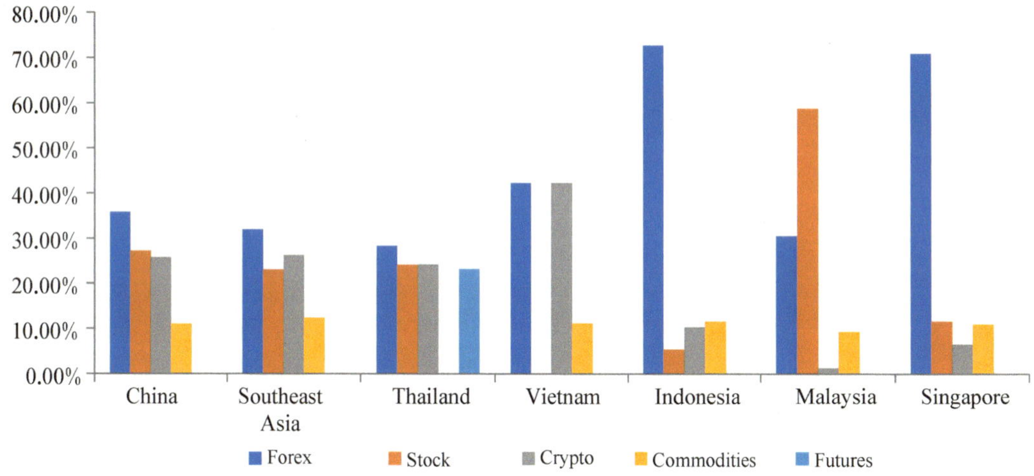

Figure 2-21: 2019 Investor's Trading Preferences in China and Southeast Asia

Source: TradingView.

4. IC Markets Outperforms in Southeast Asia

According to the data from Followme, IC Markets has a strong performance among brokers in Southeast Asia in 2019, with both the number of accounts and trading volume ranking first, and the number of active users ranking second. In addition to IC Markets, XM, FBS, FxPro, Pepperstone, and Charterprime have all entered the top 10 rankings in terms of account numbers, active users, and trading volume.

Table 2-1: 2019 Top10 Brokers in Southeast Asia

Top10	Southeast Asia
Account Numbers	IC Markets、XM、FBS、FxPro、Pepperstone、TradeMax、Charterprime、AvaTrade、FXTM、AxiTrader
Active Users	XM、ICMarkets、FBS、FxPro、Charterprime、Pepperstone、USGFX、AvaTrade、Exness、FXTM
Trading Volume	ICMarkets、USGFX、TradeMax、XM、RoboForex、Charterprime、FBS、Pepperstone、FxPro、Forex.com

Source: Followme.

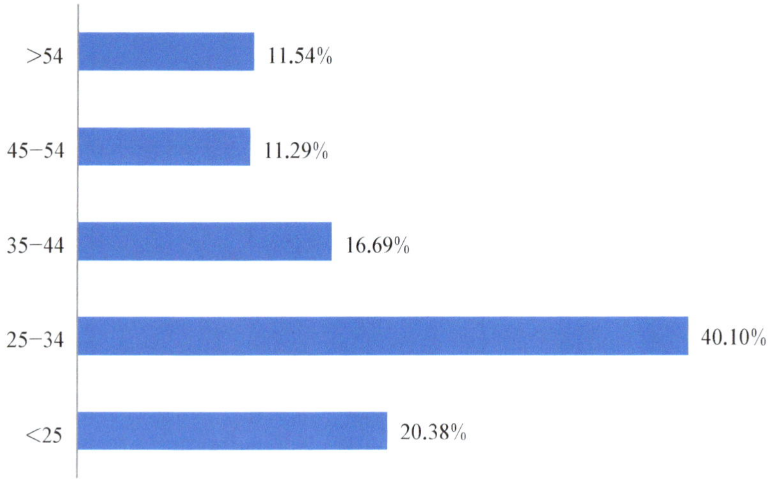

2019 Foreign Exchange and Precious Metals Market Blue Book

Age	Percentage
>54	11.54%
45−54	11.29%
35−44	16.69%
25−34	40.10%
<25	20.38%

Figure 2–18: Age Distribution of Investors in Southeast Asia in 2019
Source: TradingView.

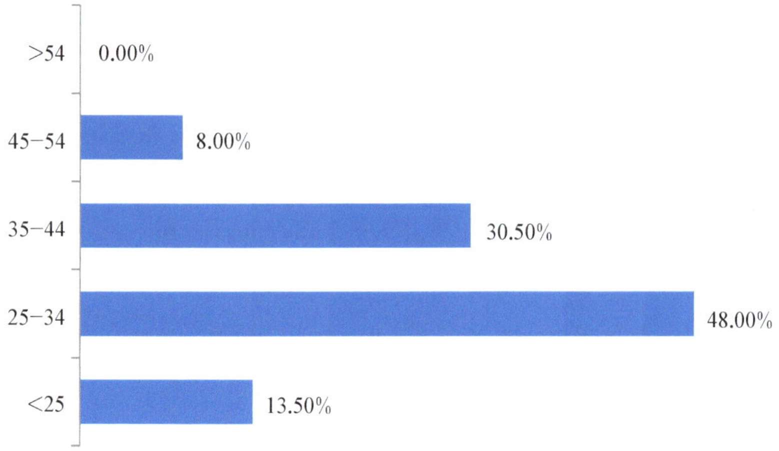

Age	Percentage
>54	0.00%
45−54	8.00%
35−44	30.50%
25−34	48.00%
<25	13.50%

Figure 2–19: Age Distribution of Investors in Southeast Asia in 2019
Source: Followme.

2. Southeast Asian Investors Also Prefer Ultra-short-term Trading

According to data from the Followme, 92.51% of transactions are ultra-short-term transactions, and transactions within the week and more than one week account for 5.77% and 1.73%, respectively.

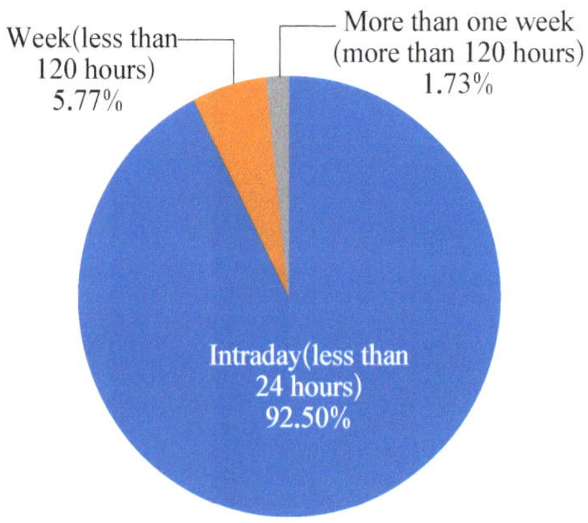

Week(less than 120 hours) 5.77%
More than one week (more than 120 hours) 1.73%
Intraday(less than 24 hours) 92.50%

Figure 2–20: Investor Positions Distribution in Southeast Asia in 2019
Source: Followme.

（Ⅱ）Southeast Asia

1. Southeast Asian Investors are Also Mainly Male, and the Main Age Group is Also 25–34

According to Tradingview data, men accounted for 78.7% of investors in the Southeast Asian market, which is the absolute main force. Followme's data also shows that men account for 98.64% and women account for only 1.04%.

In terms of age, both communities show that the main age group of investors in Southeast Asia is 25–34, which is consistent with the distribution of investors in China. The second-ranked age group is 35–44, which is different from the distribution of investors in China. Among them, investors aged 25–34 account for 48% in Followme, 40.1% in TradingView. The proportions of investors aged 35–44 are 30.5% and 16.69%, respectively.

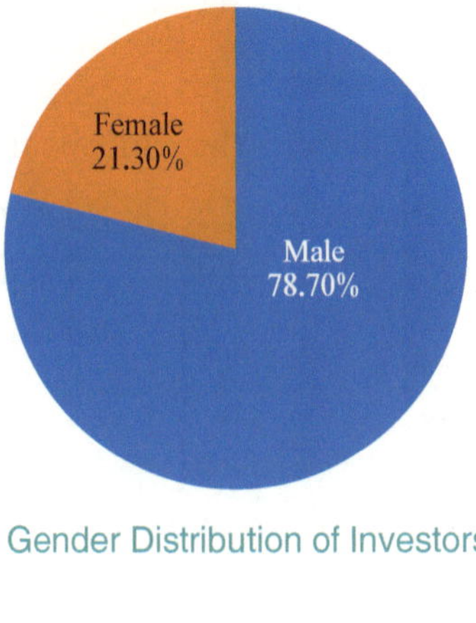

Figure 2-17: 2019 Gender Distribution of Investors in Southeast Asia

Source: TradingView.

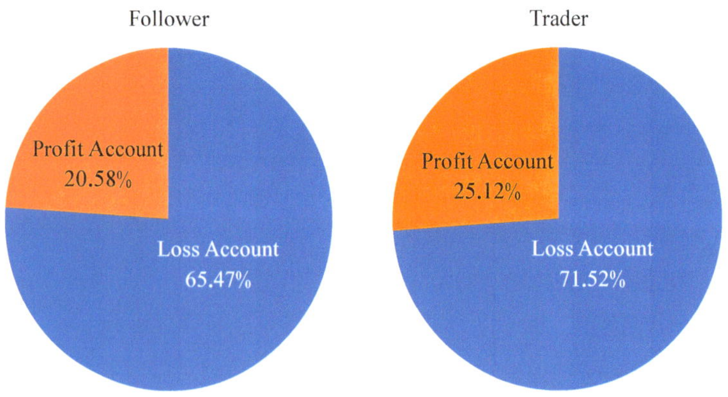

2019 Foreign Exchange and Precious Metals Market Blue Book

Figure 2–16: 2019 Profit and Loss Account Distribution. Left Followers and Right Traders.
Source: Followme.

profit account was 20.58%, a slightly lower than traders', and the net-loss account accounted for 65.47%. This was mainly because followers still had some independent trading orders.

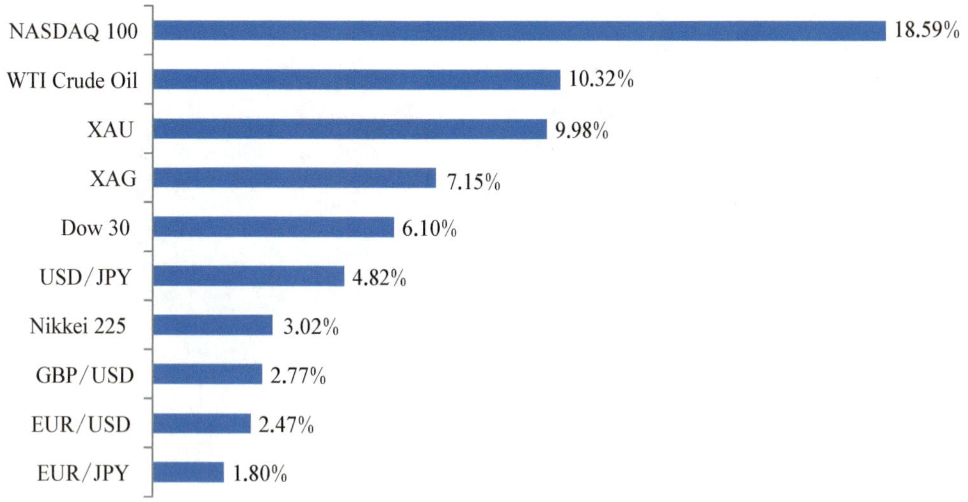

Part 2 Retail Investor Structure and Behavior in Forex Markets in China and Southeast Asia

NASDAQ 100 — 18.59%
WTI Crude Oil — 10.32%
XAU — 9.98%
XAG — 7.15%
Dow 30 — 6.10%
USD/JPY — 4.82%
Nikkei 225 — 3.02%
GBP/USD — 2.77%
EUR/USD — 2.47%
EUR/JPY — 1.80%

Figure 2-14: 2019 Top Trading Products (Real account identification data)

Soure: FX168 TradeKing.

shows that the trading volume of EUR/USD and GBP/USD was greater, in Followme, these two pairs ranked second and third in terms of trading volume, accounting for 11.54% and 8.64%, respectively. In FX168 TradeKing, the rank of these two pairs was ninth and eighth, respectively.

6. Proportion of Profitable Accounts

Data from FX168 TradeKing shows that, for users who traded on the platform, profitable accounts accounted for 37.07% and net-loss accounts accounted for 61.57%, the performance was better than the Two Eight Law. This was correlated with the upgrade of the TradeKing's trading ability and the guidance of trading performance evaluation. There are two sets of TradeKing, one is a upgrade system for quantitative trading capabilities, which helps users to form quantitative trading habits. The other is a trading performance evaluation system. By evaluating each trading of the investor, it intelligently helps users find the advantages and disadvantages of the trading, and provides an optimization plan for the disadvantages. These two systems are of great help to investors in forming good trading habits.

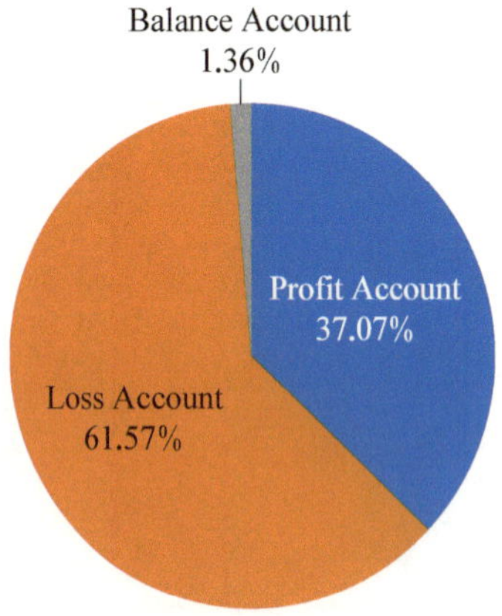

Data from Followme showed that, among traders, the profit account accounted for 25.12% and the loss account accounted for 71.52%. Among followers, the

Balance Account 1.36%
Profit Account 37.07%
Loss Account 61.57%

Figure 2-15: Profit and Loss Account Distribution in 2019

Source: FX168 TradeKing.

29

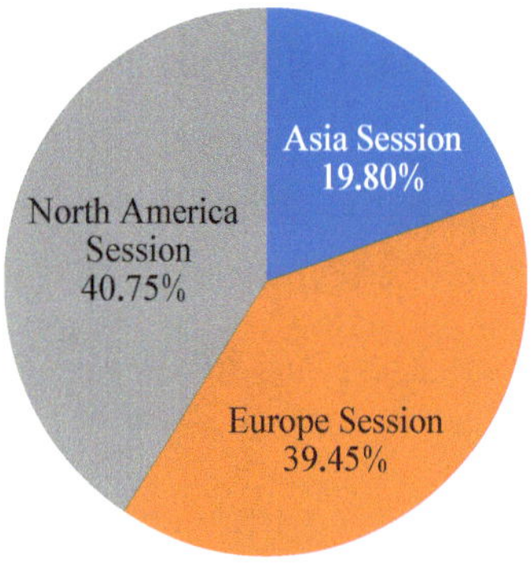

2019 Foreign Exchange and Precious Metals Market Blue Book

Figure 2-12: 2019 Chinese Investor Trading Hour Distribution (Real Account Identification Data)

Source: FX168 TradeKing.

In addition, from the data of FX168 TradeKing, it can be seen that 80% of transactions in 2019 were taking place in Europe and North American Session. This is related to the important event of 2019: Brexit and the Sino-US trade war continue to develop but without result. In terms of specific data, the trading volume in the European and the North American session was similar, accounting for 39.45% and 40.75% respectively, and the Asian session was 19.8%.

5. Chinese Investors Prefer to Trade Spot Gold and WTI Crude Oil, Other Trading Targets Have Different Preferences

In Followme, the largest trading volume in 2019 was spot gold, accounting for 26.7%, and WTI crude oil ranked fourth, accounting for 2.77%. In FX168 TradeKing, WTI crude oil and spot gold ranked second and third, accounting for 10.32% and 9.98% respectively. It is worth noting that the Nasdaq 100 Index was the number one trading objective in the FX168 TradeKing's real account identification data, showing that stock index CFD products were also quite popular with investors to a certain extent.

For forex trading currency pairs, data from Followme and FX168 TradeKing all

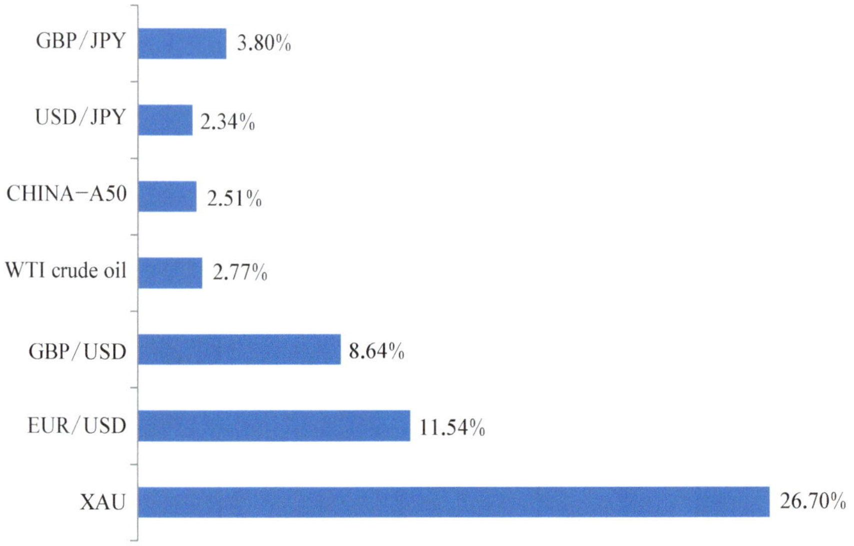

Figure 2-13: 2019 Top Trading Products

Source: Followme.

28

Part 2 Retail Investor Structure and Behavior in Forex Markets in China and Southeast Asia

Data from FX168 TradeKing shows that Guangdong Province has become the province with the highest proportion of users in 2019, accounting for 15.05%. Data from the Followme also show that in 2019, the proportion of users from Guangdong Province in China was the highest, reaching 41.07%.

Data from FX168 TradeKing also shows that although the proportion of users in central Hubei Province in 2019 still ranks second, the proportion of users has fallen significantly, from 24.5% in 2018 to 10.96%.

In Followme, followed by Guangdong Province are Shandong Province and Jiangsu Province, and Hubei Province is only ranked seventh.

4. Chinese Investors Prefer Ultra-short-term Trading, and the Trading Volume in Europe and North American Session is Similar

Data from FX168 TradeKing and Followme shows that, ultra short-term trading (opening and closing positions on the same day) ranked first in terms of transaction volume. The ultra-short-term trading volume of Followme accounts for 88.03%, which is much higher than the 50% of FX168 TradeKing. In FX168 TradeKing, the trading volume of short-term and mid-term transactions is 40.88%. This is related to the FX168 Finance College continuing to provide more systematic training courses in 2019 and encourage students to master more systematic trading methods. At the same time, it also shows that although forex trading is a class of transactions with heavy speculative attributes, if you have mastered the appropriate trading methods, you can still patiently hold long positions and execute mid-term trades.

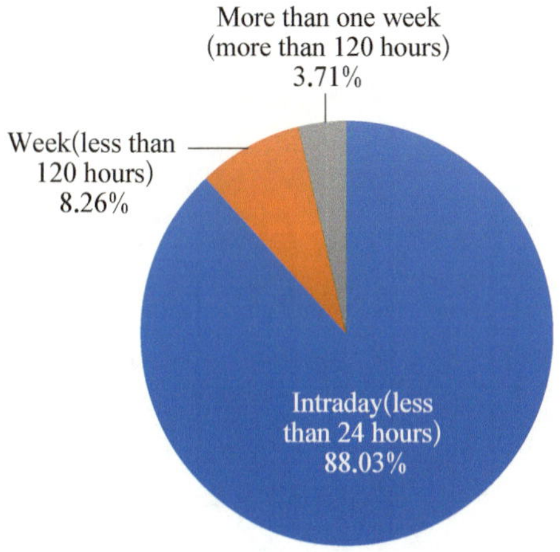

Figure 2–10: 2019 Chinese Investor Positions Distribution

Source: Followme.

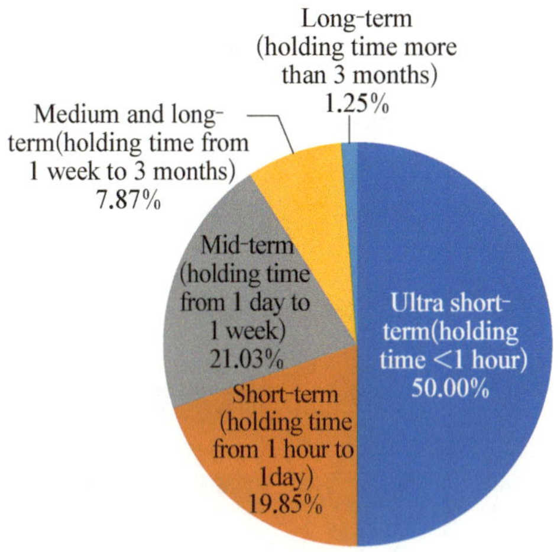

Figure 2–11: 2019 Chinese Investor Positions Distribution (Real Account Identification Data)

Source: FX168 TradeKing.

years old. In Followme, the proportion of this age group reached 52.13%, in TradingView was 41.26%, and in FX168 TradeKing was 40.91%.

In FX168 TradeKing, another age group with a high proportion is 18–24 years old, accounting for 41.32%, which is slightly higher than 25–34 age group. It is also the highest proportion among these 3 communities. The second-ranking age group in the Followme and Tradingview are 35–44.

3. Chinese Investors are Most Concentrated in Guangdong Province, and the Proportion of Users in Hubei Province has Dropped Significantly

FX168 TradeKing and Followme provide geographical distribution of Chinese investors, data shows that the most concentrated Chinese investors in 2019 are Guangdong Province.

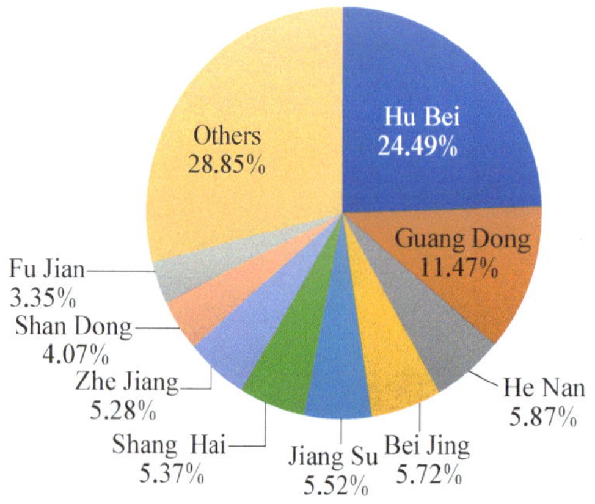

Figure 2–7: Chinese Investor Geographical Distribution in 2018

Source: FX168 TradeKing.

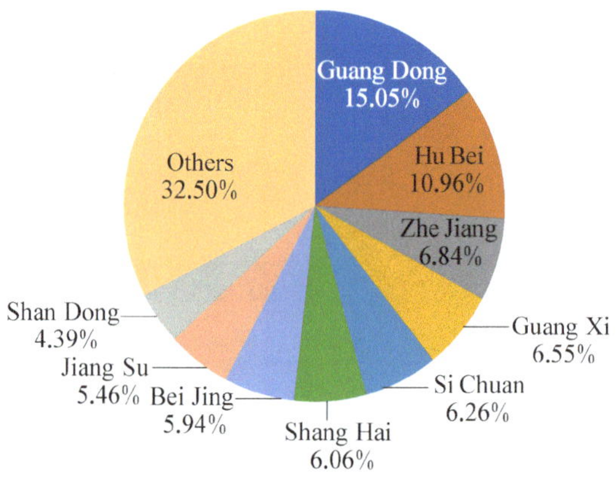

Figure 2–8: Chinese Investor Geographical Distribution in 2019

Source: FX168 TradeKing.

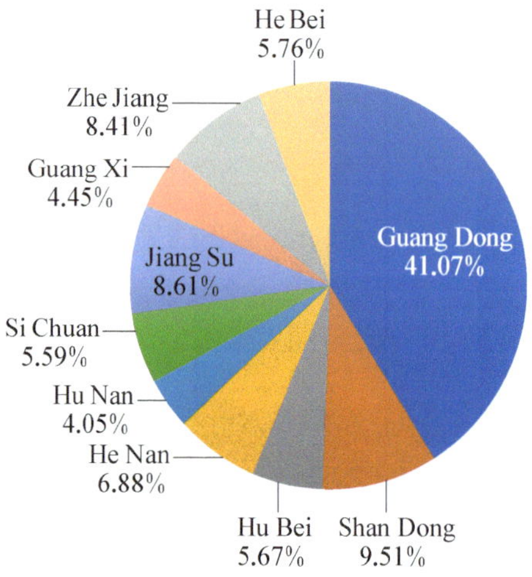

Figure 2–9: 2019 Chinese Investor Geographical Distribution

Source: Followme.

Part 2   Retail Investor Structure and Behavior in Forex Markets in China and Southeast Asia

2. Among Chinese Investors, the 25–34 Age Groups are the Main Force, and the Second Main Age Group Show Differentiation among Different Platforms

Data from three communities shows that among investors, the main age group is 25–34

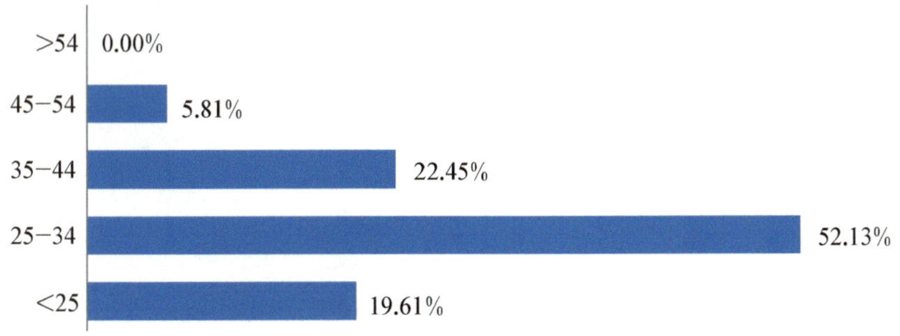

Figure 2–4: 2019 Chinese Investor Age Distribution

Source: Followme.

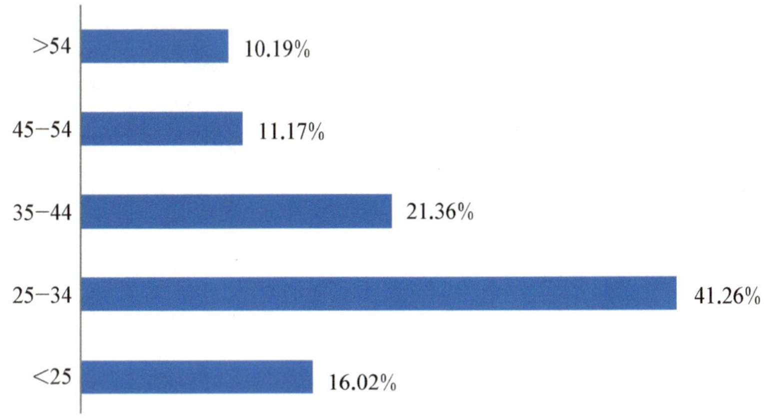

Figure 2–5: 2019 Chinese Investor Age Distribution

Source: TradingView.

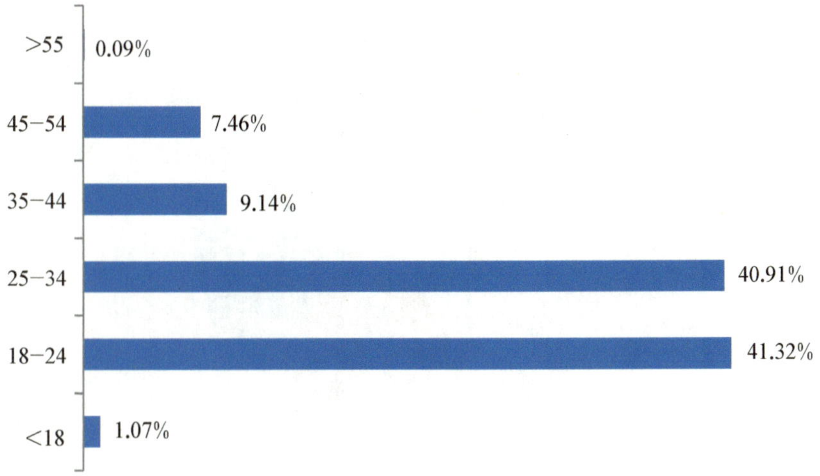

Figure 2–6: 2019 Chinese Investor Age Distribution

Source: FX168 TradeKing.

（Ⅰ） China

1. Males are the Absolute Dominant Force among Chinese Investors, with Data from One Community Showing Males Being Extremely High

Among Chinese investors in 2019, men are the main force, and one of the three communities shows that men account for 97.45%. The data shows that the ratio of male to female in the FX168 TradeKing and TradingView is roughly 8：2. According to the data from the Followme, 97.45% are male, and only 2.55% are female.

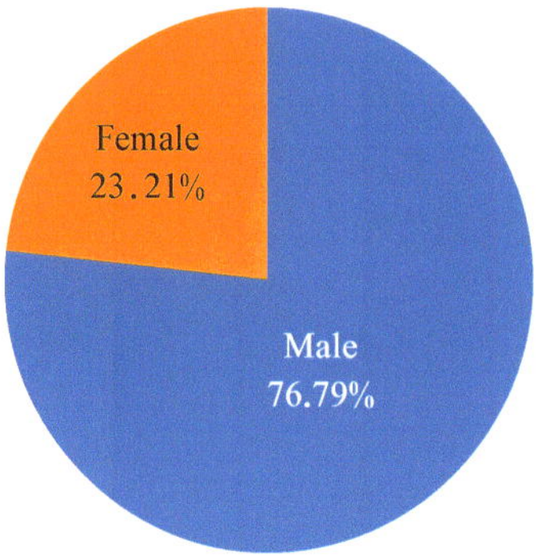

Figure 2-1: 2019 Chinese Investor Gender Distribution

Source: FX168 TradeKing.

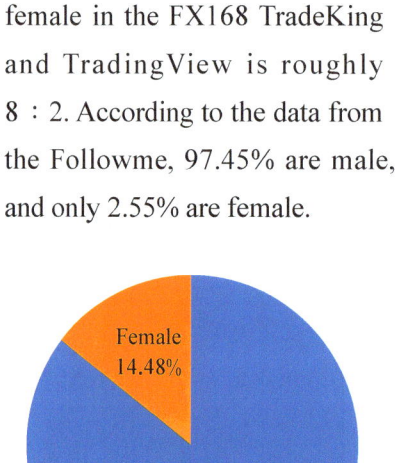

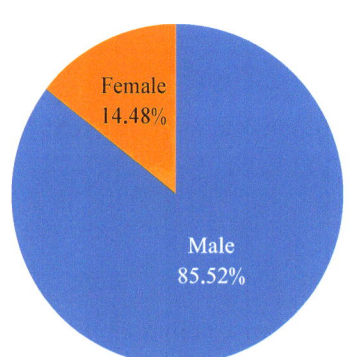

Figure 2-2: 2019 Chinese Investor Gender Distribution

Source: TradingView.

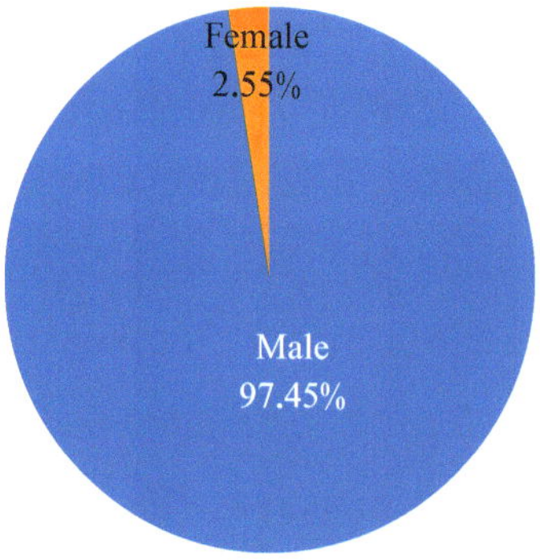

Figure 2-3: 2019 Chinese Investor Gender Distribution

Source: Followme.

Part **2**

Retail Investor Structure and Behavior in Forex Markets in China and Southeast Asia

In order to fully understand the retail investor structure and analyze investor trading behavior, FX168 Finance Group collects data in different forms each year to further study the industry and explore the direction of the industry's development. This time we added research on the Southeast Asian market. There are three main sources of data: FX168 TradeKing community and its real account identification data, trading community Followme and TradingView. The data in this Part covers the period from January 1, 2019 to December 31, 2019. Special thanks to the institutions for their participation and support for the FX168 Blue Book.

Commission announced that starting from January 1, 2020, the restrictions on the foreign shareholding ratio of futures companies will be lifted, and eligible investors can hold 100% of shares. Restrictions on foreign ownership of fund management companies and securities companies will also be lifted on April 1, 2020 and December 1, 2020, respectively.

October 25, 2019, the People's Bank of China and the European Central Bank renewed a bilateral domestic currency swap agreement with a swap size of 350 billion RMB/45 billion Euros. The agreement is valid for three years and can be extended upon mutual agreement.

November 19, 2019, the China Foreign Exchange Trading Center and the Moscow Exchange signed a memorandum of understanding aimed at increasing the mechanism for the direct exchange price of the RMB to the Ruble and promoting the settlement of bilateral domestic currencies.

December 5, 2019, the People's Bank of China and the Macau Monetary Authority signed a bilateral local currency swap agreement to maintain financial stability and support the economic and financial development of the two places. The scale of the agreement is 30 billion RMB/35 billion MOP. The agreement is valid for three years and can be extended upon mutual agreement.

Note: Historical data on the development of China's foreign exchange market can be found in the FX168 blue book over the years.

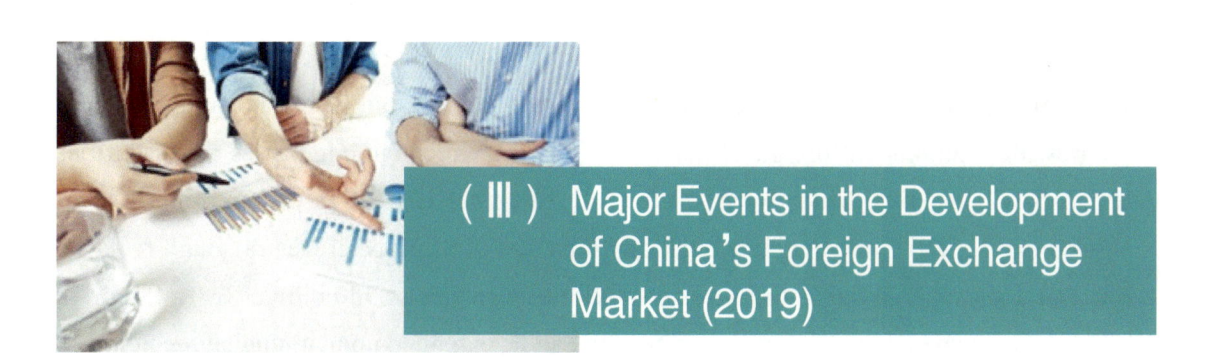

（Ⅲ） Major Events in the Development of China's Foreign Exchange Market (2019)

February 11, 2019, the People's Bank of China and the Central Bank of Suriname renewed a bilateral domestic currency swap agreement of 1 billion RMB/1.1 billion Surinamese.

May 10, 2019, the People's Bank of China and the Monetary Authority of Singapore renewed a bilateral domestic currency swap agreement with a scale of 300 billion RMB/61 billion Singapore dollars.

May 30, 2019, the People's Bank of China and the Turkish Central Bank renewed a bilateral domestic currency swap agreement with a scale of 12 billion RMB/10.9 billion Turkish lira.

June 5, 2019, the RMB Qualified Foreign Institutional Investor (RQFII) pilot area was expanded to the Netherlands, with an investment quota of 50 billion RMB.

June 17, 2019, the Shanghai-London Stock Connect was officially launched. The Shanghai-London Stock Connect refers to the interconnection mechanism between the Shanghai Stock Exchange and the London Stock Exchange.

August 6, 2019, the US Treasury listed China as a "currency manipulator."

September 10, 2019, China's State Administration of Foreign Exchange announced the cancellation of the investment quota restrictions for QFII and RQFII.

October 11, 2019, the China Securities Regulatory

monthly performance in more than a year. In contrast, other Asian countries still maintain an open attitude towards cryptocurrencies.

In 2019, South Korea has taken an important step towards regulating the cryptocurrency space. On November 27, 2019, the National Policy Committee of the South Korean National Assembly passed a bill allowing effective regulation of cryptocurrencies, but the legislative process has not yet been completed. The new bill officially classifies cryptocurrencies as digital assets and classifies cryptocurrency exchanges as regulated financial companies. This is an important step for South Korea. According to the Bank of Korea, South Korean exchanges hold about $1.9 billion worth of cryptocurrencies.

On the other hand, the Malaysian Securities Commission (SC) has also started to approve eligible exchanges to provide digital asset trading services in Malaysia, and the cryptocurrency exchange Luno has become the first cryptocurrency exchange to receive such approval from the Malaysian regulatory authority.

Luno CEO Marcus Swanepoel said:"We are seeing a revolution in the use of cryptocurrencies in global financial services, but this is not an overnight change. Regulators like the Malaysian Securities Commission's research on new digital assets and blockchain technology Show leadership in this area."

Similarly, in order to promote the growth of digital assets, the Thailand Securities and Exchange Commission also said that it is planning to amend the Royal Decree against the industry in 2020. The regulator has reportedly begun researching various obstacles in the decree. The decree came into effect in 2018 and affects businesses related with digital assets.

Ruenvadee Suwanmongkol, Secretary General of the Thai Securities and Exchange Commission, told local media:"Regulators must flexibly apply rules and regulations in accordance with the market environment. For example, laws should not be outdated and should serve market needs, especially for new digital asset products, and compete with global markets. We need to explore any possible obstacles."

2017. The new shutdown and restrictions were the largest rectification the industry has encountered since the first rectification in September 2017. Almost a year ago, China blocked more than 120 offshore cryptocurrency exchanges that provided trading services to mainland citizens. Also in early November 2019, the People's Bank of China's Shanghai headquarters disclosed its intention to crack down on cryptocurrency transactions. The central bank urges all banks to abide by Chinese laws and refrain from engaging in cryptocurrency transactions. It stated that relevant departments will also continue to monitor and close domestic websites related to cryptocurrency transactions and ICOs, and prohibit payment services from accepting cryptocurrencies.

Increasing scrutiny also caused bitcoin's value to plummet in November 2019, its worst

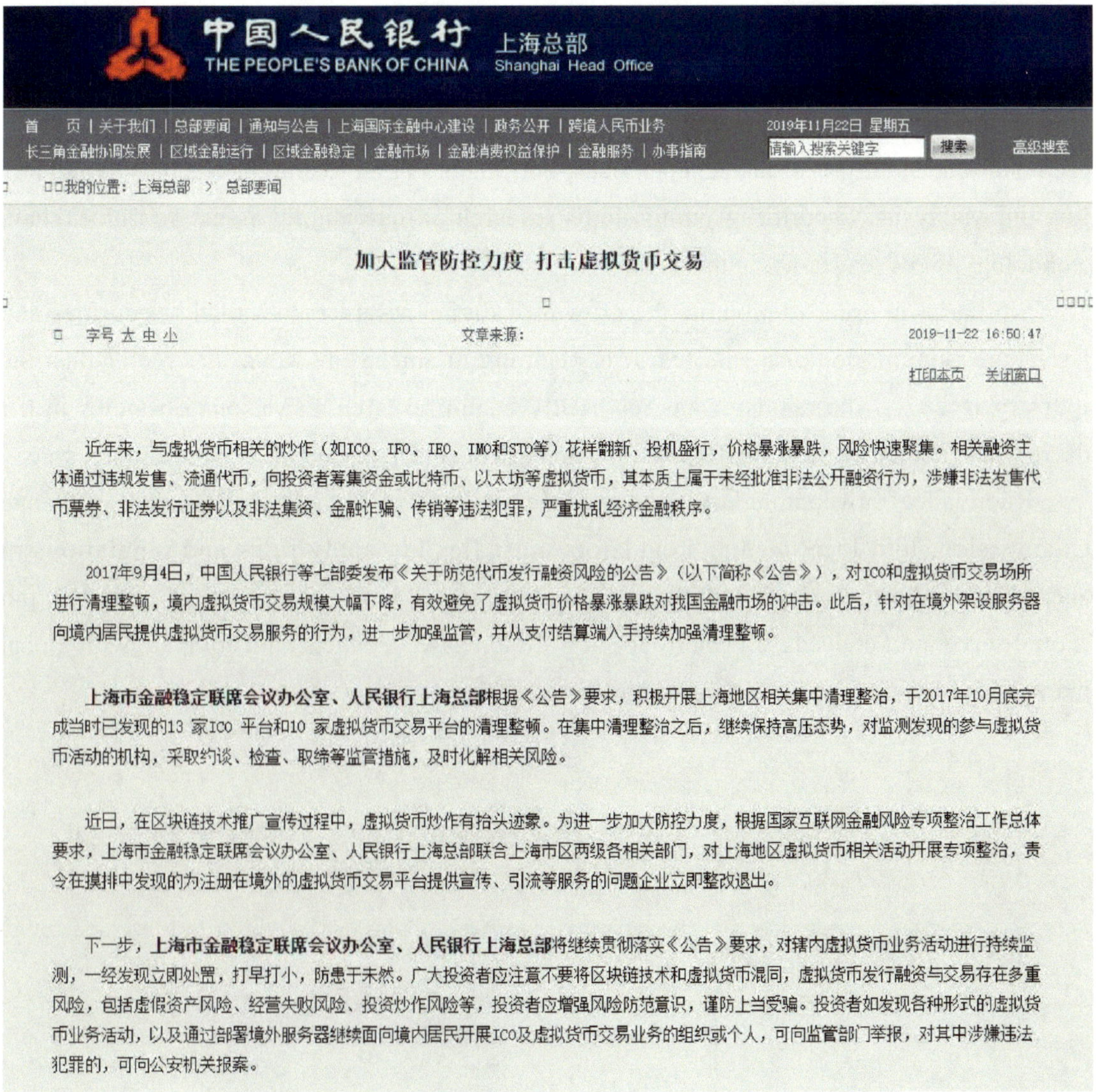

Picture 1-5: Announcement of the People's Bank of China

would pay full reserves to the central bank, the digital currency of the central bank is still the debt of the central bank, which is guaranteed by the credit of the central bank, and has unlimited legality.

In addition, Mu Changchun also emphasized that at this stage, the central bank's digital currency design focuses on M0 (replacement of banknotes and coins instead of M1 and M2). For the question of whether to adopt blockchain technology, at the level of the central bank, technology neutrality should be maintained, no technical route pre-set, and not necessarily relying on a certain technical route.

Mu Changchun said, we are currently in a race, several designated operating agencies take different technical routes for R & D of DC/EP, the winner will eventually be accepted by the people and the market. So this is the process of market competition and selection.

Fan Yifei, deputy governor of the People's Bank of China, said at the "8th China Payment and Clearing Forum" on November 28, 2019, at present, the central bank's legal digital currency DC/EP basically completes the top-level design, standard formulation, functional research and development, joint debugging and testing. The next step will be to select a trial verification area, scenario and service scope reasonably, and steadily promote the introduction and application of digital form of legal currency.

However, with the development of China's central bank's legal digital currency, various false rumors in the market are endless. At the end of 2019, the central bank also issued a document to address rumors specifically, urging the general public to raise risk awareness and to prevent damage of interests.

Huang Qifan, deputy director of the China International Economic Exchange Center and Huang Yiping, deputy dean of the Peking University National Development Research Institute, said that the People's Bank of China is likely to become the first central bank in the world to launch digital currencies. Therefore, some people speculate that 2020 will become the first year of China's legal digital currency.

3. Asian Countries Have Different Attitudes towards Cryptocurrencies, China Remains the Strictest

With the launch of the statutory cryptocurrency of the People's Bank of China, the sound of various blockchain concepts and cryptocurrency trading in China is heating up. In response, the Chinese regulatory authorities have adopted a clear warning and prohibition.

It is reported that in 2019, relevant Chinese institutions have ordered at least 5 cryptocurrency exchanges to stop trading and immediately notified domestic users that they have been shut down, which was the most severe crackdown action taken by China since

Part 1   Global Foreign Exchange and Cryptocurrency Industry Hot News and Trends

U.S. lawmakers' concerns about Libra are not just for Facebook. Will a cryptocurrency such as Libra that will be used in a very wide range endanger the status of the US dollar? Will the security of the entire financial system be threatened because control of this currency is in the hands of a few private companies? Regarding these, Facebook has repeatedly promised, but the specific measures to prevent it cannot be trusted by the legislators who determine the direction of the country's development.

Not long ago, three legislative proposals in the United States attracted attention: prohibiting tech giants from entering the financial industry, stable currencies are securities (cryptocurrencies linked to price-stabilized legal tender), and prohibiting the listing of certain securities. Some analysts said that if these three bills are passed, no large technology company can issue cryptocurrencies, all stable currencies are defined as securities (not currencies), and any company that benefits from stable currencies may face the risk of being delisted.

Although Zuckerberg expressed his deep affection for Libra at the hearing:"I believe this needs to be established" and "we have reason to care about it", he also promised that Libra will never be issued before the regulators approve it. He even said that if the Libra Association, which is controlled by multiple companies, disregards the decision of the governing body to issue Libra privately, Facebook will withdraw from the Libra Association.

Zuckerberg made it clear that if Libra fails to pass regulation, it will not be issued. As of now, US regulators have not made clear whether Libra can be issued. However, the technical development of this project is proceeding normally. Its test network has been launched on September 17, 2019, and 7 nodes have been deployed. The specific node operator information has not yet been announced. In addition, 11 wallets and multiple browsers are ready.

Whether we can see Libra in 2020, we still need to wait and see.

2. 2020 is the First Year of China's Legal Digital Currency?

Unlike Libra, the pace of the launch of the People's Bank of China's legal digital currency has been fast and stable. At the 3rd China Finance Forty Forum on August 10, 2019, Mu Changchun, CF40 Special Invited Member, Deputy Director of Payment and Settlement Department of the People's Bank of China, said, "The research on the central bank's digital currency has been underway for five years from 2014 to the present. Since last year, the relevant staff of the Digital Currency Research Institute always work overtime to develop related systems, the central bank's digital currency now can be said it's ready to go."

Regarding the impact of the two-tier operating system on monetary policy, Mr. Mu said, it will not change the relationship of currency debts and debts in circulation. In order to ensure that the central bank's digital currency is not over-issued, commercial institutions

(II) Hot News in 2019 Global Cryptocurrency Market

In 2019, the most focused on the global cryptocurrency market is Libra from the United States and the legal digital currency of the People's Bank of China.

1. Libra Faces Lots of Difficulties, Regulators Have Many Doubts

According to the original plan, the first half of 2020 is the period when Libra will be officially launched. However, at present, this much-watched cryptocurrency has not been released by the United States regulators.

Facebook founder Zuckerberg emphasized the risk of "no innovation" on the digital currency track at the US Congress hearing on Libra in Oct. 2019 and actively "marketing" to Congress. Zuckerberg said:"when we are debating about Libra, the rest of the world did not wait. Libra will be supported primarily by the US dollar, and I believe it will expand the financial leadership of the United States, as well as our democratic values and global regulation. If the United States does not innovate, our financial leadership will not be guaranteed."

Libra's proposal has a great impact on the world, and many central banks have accelerated the process of issuing digital currencies since then. But within the United States, there is still a lot of oppositions to Libra.

Part 1　Global Foreign Exchange and Cryptocurrency Industry Hot News and Trends

KVB put an emphasis on its public half year's fiscal report that unpredictable supervision policies and tightened trading rules contributed to this lower-than-expected performance.

For some of the other brokers, the specific influencing factors were not stated in their brokers' published reports, but their trading volumes also decreased significantly compared with the same period last year.

GMO: Total trading volumes of first three quarters of FY2019 was registered as 5,400 billion dollars, down by 18% from 6,600 billion dollars registered a year before.

Gain Capital: The average OTC trading volume of Gain Capital during first three quarters of FY2019 was around 471.5 billion dollars. By calculations, if the final quarter continued to be registered with average performance, the total trading volume of FY2019 could be expected to be 1,900 billion dollars, which compared to FY2018 however, was achieved within a shorter period of first three quarters. Net revenue for the three quarters of FY2019 also decreased 35% to 180.6 million dollars.

Although the two challenges broadly influenced brokers' performances in FY2019, companies still managed to expand new opportunities to strengthen their marketplaces. Take IG for instance, the successful entry into US market steadily made its market share slightly increase during H2 FY2019, while CMC Markets setup a branch in German as its core EU operation hub for post-Brexit demand. Besides, the company's partnership with AZ Bank also boost its total client numbers by 500 thousand last year.

9. Challenges and Opportunities of Brokerages in FY 2019

The two common challenges–lower market volatility and tightening regulations, which numerous brokers have simultaneously mentioned quarterly or annually in their fiscal report of financial year (FY) 2019, —have imposed larger negative effect on their trading volumes and other key performance indicators. This should however change over the first half of FY2020.

Regarding lower market volatility, both JP. Morgan and Deutsche Bank sent out reports in 2019, saying their monitored CVIX index fell to the lowest level since the end of Year 2014, making no FX brokers escape the dilemma. In the report, a further discussion by Deutsche Bank concluded that five macro tangibles, ranging from period stagnant inflation, limited monetary policies, patchy economic data, uncertainties of Brexit to trade war, especially between U.S. and China, are the major push hands of extremely low volatility in the financial market.

Apart from that, the impact of tightened regulation in the foreign exchange industry is also highlighted being the second reason cutting brokers' performance of FY19.

Now, let's have a close look below at how the two factors mentioned became the headache.

IG: Subject to ESMA's restrictions and subdued market condition of H2 FY19 ending on May 30th, 2019, the net trading income of IG of FY 2019 was down by 16% to 476.9 million pounds while operating profit decreases to 192.9 million pounds, a 31% drop year-over-year. The latest released report of FY 2020 H1, however, indicated no improvement of such plight, as the net trading income was registered at 249.9 million pounds, just shy of last year's and operating profit shrank a further 10% to 100 million pounds.

CMC Markets: Similarly, the net revenue of CMC Market throughout FY2019 was down 30% to 130.8 million pounds, with total accounts and active accounts down 6% and 10% separately. Nevertheless, during the first half of FY2020 ending on Sep. 30th, 2019, CMC's net revenue went up 45% against the same period of last year to 102.3 million pounds, pretty close to the figure of the whole FY2019's. In response to this, CMC explained that customers were gradually on board with ESMA's new regulations, and continuously having sustained interests in the offered products and trading platform.

KVB: The prohibition from ASIC that Australia brokers without abroad licenses stop oversea business made KVB compulsorily close all client accounts in the mainland China of Australia subsidiary last year, resulting in a tragic slump of 95.5% in total revenue to only 1.61 million dollars, and net loss of 9.93 million dollars in H1 FY19 ending on June 2019.

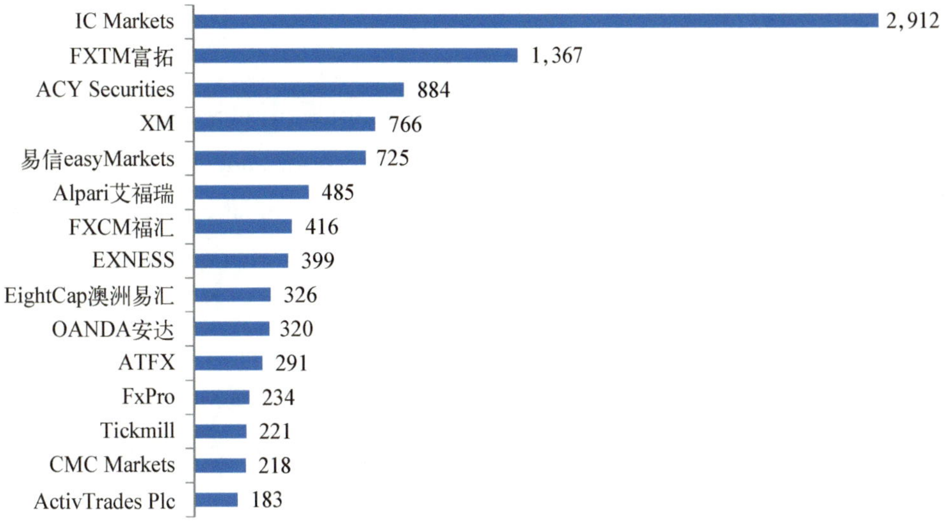

Part 1　Global Foreign Exchange and Cryptocurrency Industry Hot News and Trends

Figure 1-3: Top 15 Brokers with Most Positive Reviews

Source: FX168 Flagship Channel.

positive and negative reviews were almost the same high. From the negative reviews, we can see where the public dissatisfactions lied in. Hope it can be improved next year.

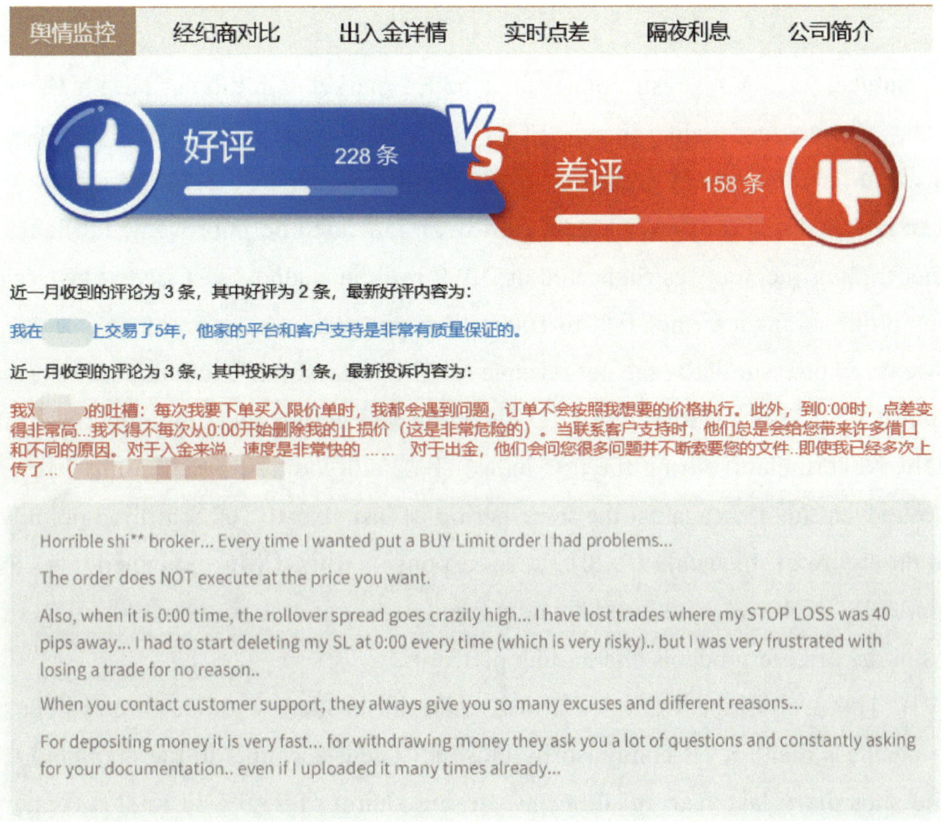

Figure 1-4: Public Opinion Monitoring Module in FX168 Flagship Channel

people on the first day was no longer as crowded as in the past, and it also made people in the industry feel "cool".

It has been 17 years since the opening of the Shanghai Money Fair. For some people, it is no longer just an exhibition—It is more like a weathervane, reflecting the prosperity of the entire industry. Based on the statistic results by FX168 Event Planning of offline financial activity data in 2019, the number of offline activities in Chinese mainland has fallen by more than 50% compared to 2018.

"Winter is here, where is the road" may become the most important issue for most brokers and practitioners in 2019. However, another data result in the survey seems to give us some answers: In 2019, the number of offline conferences and events in the mainland of China decreased 67% compared with 2018, while offline conferences and events outside of Chinese mainland, mainly on Taiwan of China and Southeast Asia increased by more than 50% compared with 2018. Market pioneers, including FX168, have set their sights on markets Taiwan of China and Southeast Asia, and those markets have become a new opportunity for all.

At the same time, according to statistics from FX168, from January to December 2019, there were 44 offline events hosted by various media in different cities in the mainland of China, and 135 offline events in 2018, decreased 67% sharply year-over-year. The industry was indeed "very cold."

8. The Public Opinion Monitoring Module from FX168 Brokers Flagship Channel Showed There Still Had Room for Brokers to Improve Their Market Reputations

In 2019, FX168 Brokers Flagship Channel received a total of 840 reviews, and many of them were complains about brokers in the industry. The complaints mainly focused on the delay of withdrawing funds, and there were also complaints about slippage and order execution.

The market reputation of a broker is a well worth attention indicator for investors. Therefore, in the fourth quarter of 2019, FX168 Brokers Flagship Channel launched a Public Opinion Monitoring Module covering all public opinions about their brokers in the internet. The Module data is updated regularly, from which we can clearly see the brokers' user base and their reputations globally.

According to the Module, as of December 31, 2019, the top 15 brokers with most positive reviews were as follows (Figure 1-3 in next page):

FX168 Monitoring Modual also showed that most of the 15 brokers mentioned above also appeared in the negative reviews rankings. To some extent it explained that these brokers' worldwide user base was big. Because there were many people using it, the numbers of

Part 1   Global Foreign Exchange and Cryptocurrency Industry Hot News and Trends

GAIN Capital
NYSE: GCAP

3.95 USD −0.10 (2.47%) ↓
12月31日 GMT-5 下午4:02

| 1D | 5D | 1M | 6M | YTD | 1Y | 5Y | MAX |

OPEN	4.05
HIGH	4.14
LOW	3.95
MARKET CAP	1.48亿
P/E RATIO	-

DIVIDEND YIELD	6.08%
PREVIOUS CLOSE	4.05
52 WEEK HIGH	7.40
52 WEEK LOW	3.75

Figure 1-2: Gain Capital's Stock Price in 2019

Source: Google.

and Exchange Commission (SEC) confirmed on November 25, 2019 that Charles Schwab was interested in acquiring TD Ameritrade. The documents show that the two companies are entering a full-stock merger and acquisition process, valued at approximately $26 billion, and the transaction is expected to be completed in the second half of 2020. Charles Schwab said this is part of its strategy. After the acquisition, Charles Schwab will add about 12 million customers, $1.3 trillion in client assets and $5 billion in annual revenue.

7. The 17th Shanghai Money Fair was Held as Scheduled, the Amount of Forex Exhibitors Reduced Drastically

On December 13–15, 2019, the 17th Shanghai Money Fair was held as scheduled. However, unlike the previous years, the organizer reduced the size of the exhibition in 2019. The West Hall of the Shanghai Exhibition Center was no longer used, and according to statistics, the total number of exhibitors was less than half of 2018. Among them, the number of forex broker exhibitors dropped significantly. On-site observations showed that the flow of

图 1.21　深证指数 2019 年表现

图 1.22　中国股指 2019 年月度收益率

的重大改革。新法明确将在中国资本市场全面推行注册制,并围绕注册制作出一系列完备的规定,设专章强调投资者权益保护。

另一方面,追逐利益的投资者认为中国的上市公司相对其他新兴市场估值仍然偏低。尤其是 2019 年前四个月的持续上扬,可以被认为是 2018 年市场急剧修正后导致估值跌入低位后的反弹。

其中电子公司表现尤其突出。京东方在 2019 年股价上升了 71%,同期内,TCL 股价上涨了 81.2%,格力电器股价上涨了 80.3%。

表 1.4　2019 年中国三大指数表现

指　　　数	恒　生	上　证	深　证	基　准
收益率(年率)	12.17%	23.72%	45.90%	18.39%
最大涨幅(月率)	11.19%(1月)	12.33%(2月)	17.54%(2月)	8.73%(1月)
最大跌幅(月率)	10.16%(5月)	3.69%(7月)	5.78%(4月)	7.37%(5月)
波动风险(月度收益率标准方差)	5.96%	4.61%	6.30%	4.63%
波动性(最高价和最低价间差值比率)	20.32%	32.72%	47.21%	20.86%

（2）印度：相对低迷　年内涨幅13.79%

印度股市指数：又称孟买敏感30指数，由孟买证券交易所发布，是最被广泛使用的股市指数，也是投资印度股市的重要指标。

图1.23　印度指数2019年表现

（3）巴西：全年涨幅27.07%　超过多数发达市场

巴西指数：圣保罗上市公司股票指数，是投资南美洲的重要指标。

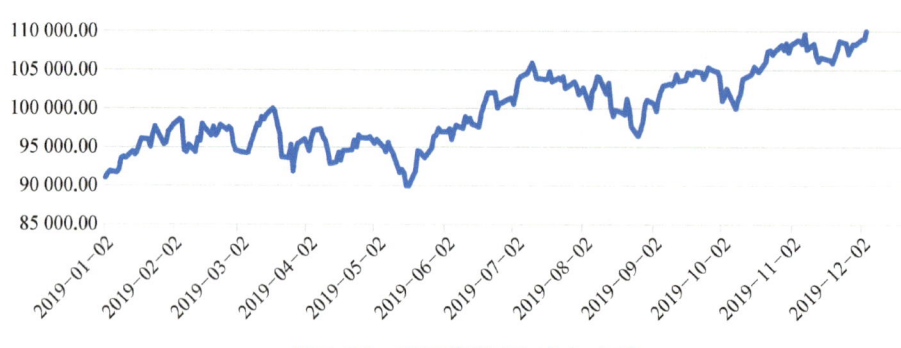

图1.24　巴西指数2019年表现

（4）俄罗斯：表现亮眼　全年上涨42.52%

俄罗斯RTS指数：由莫斯科交易所上市的50个大型公司股票构成，是俄罗斯股市重要股指之一，也是俄罗斯、东欧和许多新兴欧洲的重要指标。

图1.25　俄罗斯RTS指数2019年表现

2019年,"金砖四国"(除中国外)的另外三国股市也实现增长。其中,巴西股市表现中规中矩,收益率达到27.07%,超过多数发达市场;俄罗斯股市表现亮眼,俄罗斯RTS指数年内大幅上涨了42.52%,在本书考察的所有股指中表现仅次于深证指数;印度股市则表现相对低迷,年内只上涨了13.79%。

表1.5 "金砖四国"(除中国外)2019年股市表现

指　　　数	印　度	巴　西	俄罗斯	基　准
收益率(年率)	13.79%	27.07%	42.52%	18.39%
最大涨幅(月率)	7.23%(3月)	7.01%(1月)	11.75%(1月)	8.73%(1月)
最大跌幅(月率)	5.56%(7月)	2.33%(2月)	3.94%(8月)	7.37%(5月)
波动风险	3.71%	2.88%	4.79%	4.63%
波动性(最高价和最低价间差值比率)	17.90%	30.24%	42.57%	20.86%

印度央行在年初率先降息,3月份,股市得以反弹,当月孟买敏感30指数上涨了7.23%。但印度经济却在2019年显示疲态,四个季度的GDP增长年率明显递减(一至四季度分别为6.6%、5.8%、5%和4.5%)。即便有刺激性货币政策及财政政策的支持,该国的贫富差距巨大、财政制度缺陷等关键问题却日益凸显,导致与经济命脉相连的股市"底气不足"。

2019年,巴西和俄罗斯央行也都分别降息了4次和5次,这无疑为股市注入了巨大的动力。同时,巴西经济活力保持旺盛,尤其突出的是,巴西制造业PMI自8月份跳升以后连续4个月维持高位。俄罗斯虽然之前面临制裁,但本国企业乃至整体经济并未发生巨大震动,且在俄罗斯较为保守的政策中谋求中长期的稳定发展。分析特别指出,俄罗斯企业的资产负债表是新兴市场最为强健的一部分。

从月度收益率来看,这部分新兴市场仍和国际整体趋势保持一定的差异。在5月份全球股市大幅下滑中,这三个国家的股指仍然保持上扬。但1月份低位反弹、年内后四个月基本保持持续上涨之类的趋势与发达市场和中国股市相符。

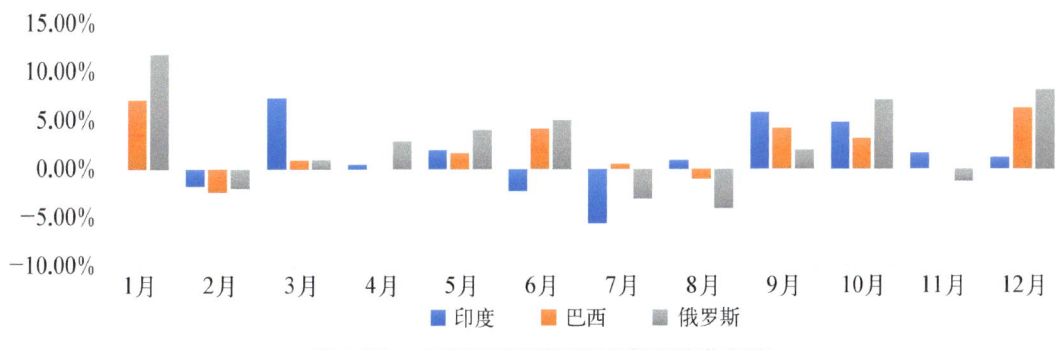

图1.26 金砖三国股指2019年月度收益率

（5）新兴市场比较

- **收益率**

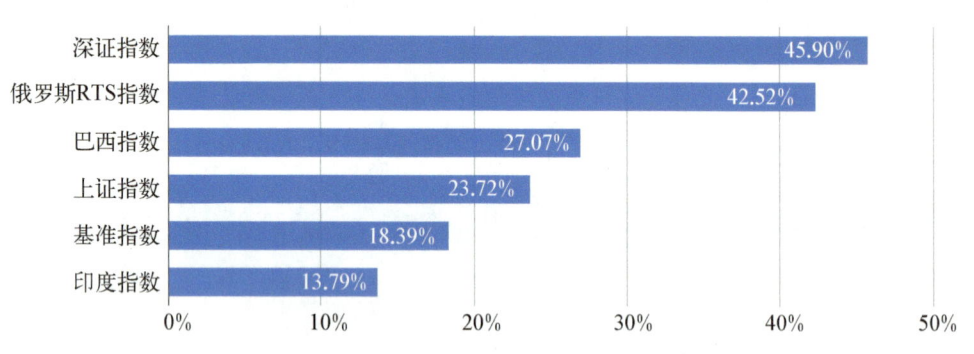

图1.27 "金砖四国"股指2019年收益率

在新兴市场比较的五个股指中，2019年收益最高的是深证指数，涨幅高达45.9%，俄罗斯RTS指数紧随其后，涨幅也达到42.52%。仅有印度指数年内收益率低于基准指数，为13.79%，这也是五只股指中唯一涨幅低于20%的。

- **波动性**

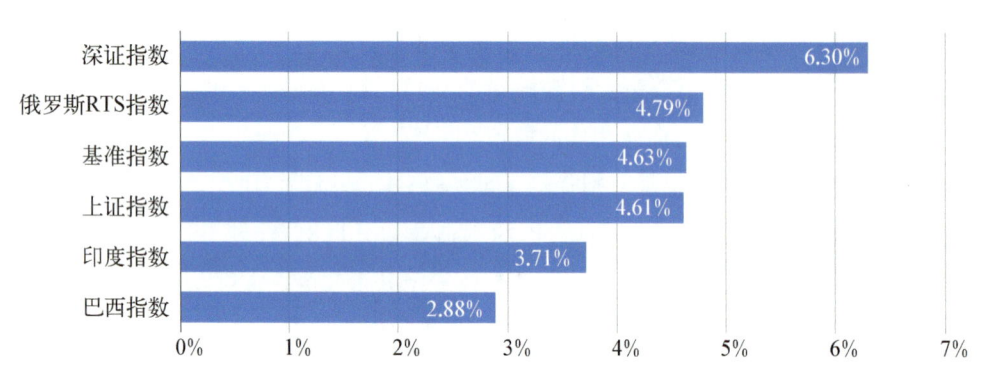

图1.28 "金砖四国"股指2019年月度收益率波动性（标准方差）

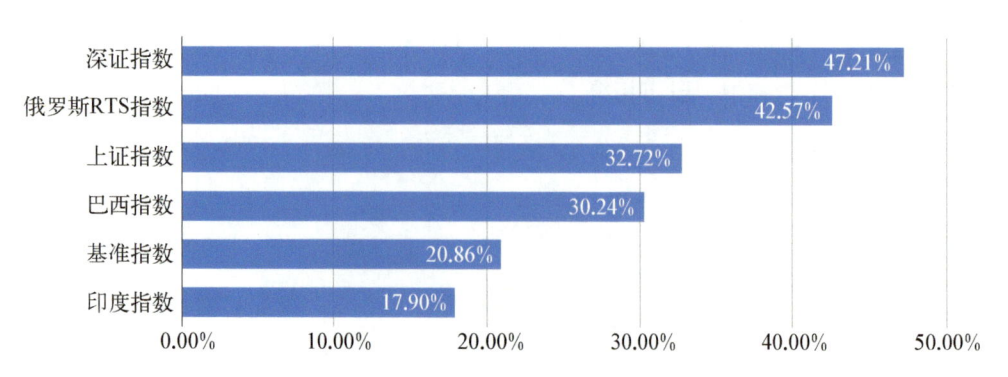

图1.29 "金砖四国"股指2019年价格波动性（最高价和最低价差值比率）

无论是以月度收益率标准方差还是极值差价比率衡量的波动性，都是深证指数和俄罗斯RTS指数最高。以前者衡量的波动性来看，最高的两个指数分别为6.3%和4.79%，均高于基准指数。其

18

余三个股指的波动性小于基准指数,巴西指数最低,为2.88%。以后者衡量的波动性来看,深证指数和俄罗斯RTS指数分别高达47.21%和42.57%,上证指数和巴西指数也都高于30%,只有印度指数的价格波动低于基准指数,为17.9%。

- 板块表现

2019年各行业股票年收益率如下:

表1.6　2019年各行业股票年收益率

MSCI	新兴市场	发达市场	世界指数
非必需消费品	30.791%	19.329%	20.880%
必需消费品	7.430%	18.279%	17.259%
能　源	11.812%	0.440%	2.196%
金　融	5.153%	18.357%	16.019%
医　疗	3.694 8%	19.550%	19.095%
信息技术	41.375%	46.650%	46.087%
工　业	2.788%	22.030%	20.798%
材　料	−0.705%	12.592%	10.200%
地　产	17.429%	15.681%	15.917%
电信服务	7.793%	21.989%	19.607%
公用事业	3.090%	16.779%	15.461%

2019年,全球股市各板块几乎全部有所上涨。非必需消费品和信息技术板块表现尤其突出。新兴市场的非必需消费品板块涨幅达到30.79%,信息技术板块在全球市场的涨幅都超过40%。

能源和材料板块则表现相对疲弱。能源板块在发达市场的涨幅仅为0.44%,材料板块在新兴市场略微收跌,下降了0.705%。

1.2 2020年全球股票市场展望

展望2020年,随着贸易战激化的风险降低,全球许多主要经济体也展现出增长复苏的迹象,各大机构对于全球风险资产仍持较为乐观的态度,但也认为2019年全球股市集体上涨两位数百分点的盛况可能难以为继。

1.2.1 上涨趋势的股票市场:中国、美国

- **中国**

许多机构都看好中国股市。在政府和央行刺激政策的支持下,分析预期中国股市或将迎来周期性反弹。

其中瑞士信贷就预期中国股指会在2020年跑赢全球新兴市场综合指数。

瑞士银行则表示,鉴于盈利前景和风险情绪改善,2020年战术性看好亚洲(日本除外)股票。其中,特别看好2020年中国股市前景,互联网和5G受益股将有不错表现。

- **美国**

专家也预期美国股市将会延续2019年的涨势,这主要是以美联储在短期内不会收紧货币政策为基础。花旗预期2020年美国股市继续上涨的概率接近90%。该公司首席美国股票策略师Tobias Levkovich在周四的彭博电视采访中称,他们的调查显示投资者笃定"美联储在2021年之前都会按兵不动",而这将推升股市。

Levkovich说道:"利率如此之低的原因是恐怕我们没有足够好的增长、恐怕我们达不到通胀目标,而你可以得到更高的股票风险溢价,部分弥补低债券收益率,所以估值会走高,显然会高于现在的。"

瑞银资产管理美国价值股部门总监Thomas Digenan在同一个采访中表示:"在这样的利率环境中,总体市场真的很具有吸引力。

我们度过了大概五年的时间,这期间投资者无法相信我们所处的利率环境。而这是真实的,我想相应的指标应该进行调整。"

但美国股市仍存在风险,这包括特朗普所主导的贸易政策的进展以及2020年进行的美国大选。即便这些风险最终都能烟消云散,美国股市已经经历了史上最长的牛市,泡沫是否已然产生以及如果产生、何时会破灭,都是摆在投资者面前严峻的问题。只能说,美国股市或许能维持上升态势,但涨幅可能会放缓,且波动性可能上升。

1.2.2 区间震荡的股票市场：欧洲、日本

- 欧洲

被认为是估值偏低的欧洲市场在仍属坚挺的经济以及宽松的货币政策环境中具有一定的上升空间。

但对于欧洲市场来说,2019年过后仍然悬而未决的除了全球瞩目的贸易关系问题,还有本土的一系列风险因素。

其中重要的一项是英国退欧。英国"脱欧"协议生效后英国于2020年1月31日进入退欧过渡期,正式成为第一个退出欧盟的国家。双方面临着更为艰难的贸易谈判。英国首相约翰逊坚称不会延长过渡期,这意味着,如果英国和欧盟无法在2020年12月31日之前达成贸易协议,英国就会无协议退欧。而从最近的案例来看,欧盟和加拿大签订贸易协议花费了七年之久,可见仅仅11个月的谈判时间对于英国和欧盟来说极为紧张。一旦英国无协议退欧,断崖式的无序退欧将对英国和欧盟双方都带来巨大的经济打击。

除了英国退欧,欧盟委员会和欧洲央行都在2019年年底换届,面临着对体制结构缺陷带来的挑战,从而需要相关的财政政策和货币政策改革。若这一进程能够加快且向积极的方面发展,则可助力股市;反之,相应的风险或令股市受阻。

另一方面,欧盟还面临意大利民粹政府、希腊政府财务以及西班牙加泰罗尼亚独立等地缘政治潜在危机,需要投资者更加谨慎。

- 日本

日本的刺激性财政政策无疑对股市是一大利好,且日本股市整体长期估值偏低,也是对投资者的吸引力之一。

但日本提高消费税的影响仍有待发酵。同时,日本央行长期实行的超级宽松货币政策导致再度发生严重震荡时有效措施极为有限。

贝莱德表示,看好日本股市,认为其将成为全球复苏的受益者,日本企业预计将从全球制造业复苏和国内财政刺激中受益,但也应注意到日本央行货币政策的调整空间不如很多央行。

因此,预期日本股市将于2020年在利多和利空因素的双方拉锯中震荡前行。

1.2.3 下跌趋势的股票市场：印度等部分新兴市场

部分具有危机的新兴市场需要投资者更为谨慎。比如委内瑞拉股市在2019年创下了超过50倍的涨幅。但当地的通货膨胀和货币贬值状况极为严重,致使由本国货币计算的股市回报率基本没有意义。

除了这种不具参考意义的经济体股市,一些新兴市场整体市值不高,波动性极大,也是希望减

小风险的投资者需要避免的。

除此之外，像印度这样虽然具有短期刺激政策，但仍有社会根本性问题需要深度改革来解决的经济体股票市场，也具有较高风险。在全球经济复苏迟缓、贸易关系仍然值得担忧的大环境下，这种市场下跌的可能性大于上涨的可能性。

1.2.4 行业推荐：非必需消费品、科技、医疗

2020年，地缘政治和贸易关系不确定性将继续施压工业和能源等行业。但从2019年的表现来看，尽管去全球化导致全球经济增长放缓，但各个主要经济体内需仍然旺盛，反映为非必需消费品板块表现出色，2020年这一趋势料将继续。

2019年表现最为亮眼的科技股更是动力十足。分析师看到这一作为人类最具创造力且站在信息时代前端的行业在可见的未来仍然潜能巨大。

另一个值得关注的板块是医疗股。全球各国老龄化的趋势以及生物科技的迅速发展使得这一行业必将在未来几十年里蓬勃发展。同时，这一行业的优势还在于，当经济下行时，通常医疗股仍能表现良好。

2

全球货币市场篇

2.1 2019年全球货币市场回顾

2019年美元再次展现出很强的韧性,虽然美联储在年内完成了三次降息,但每次降息实际上都偏向鹰派,并不足以推动美元出现实质性的长期回调,同时,贸易局势的波折不断也意外彰显出美元的避险价值,更重要的是,美国相对强势的经济表现为美元提供了一定的助力。但随着中美贸易协议在接近年底时出现积极发展,截至2019年12月31日,美元兑全球前8大主要货币中仅有3种升值,分别是兑人民币、澳元和欧元。美元指数虽然连续两年上涨,但创下了历史上最小的年度涨幅。

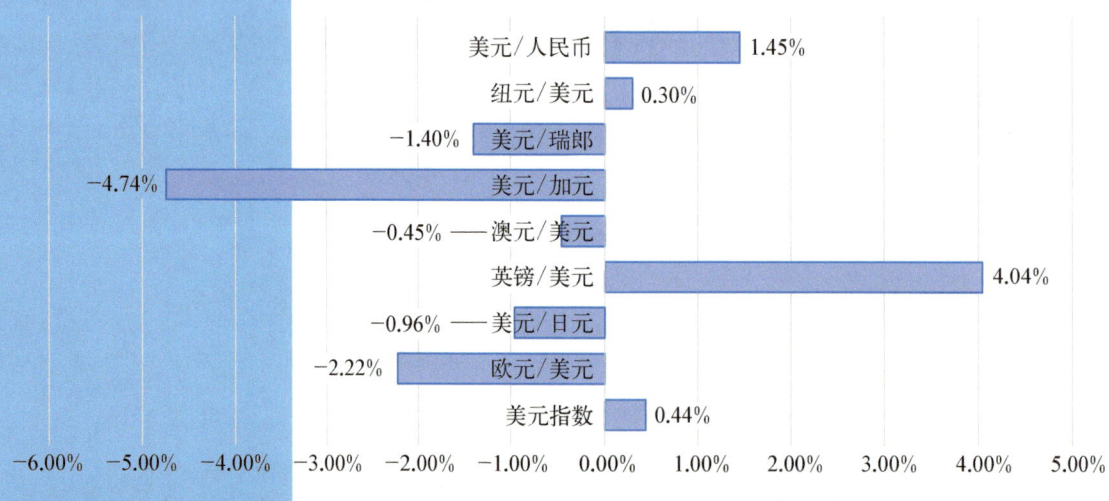

货币对	涨跌幅
美元/人民币	1.45%
纽元/美元	0.30%
美元/瑞郎	−1.40%
美元/加元	−4.74%
澳元/美元	−0.45%
英镑/美元	4.04%
美元/日元	−0.96%
欧元/美元	−2.22%
美元指数	0.44%

图2.1　2019年主要货币对表现

通过图2.1,我们可以发现,2019年内美元整体表现已经远不如2018年,其中加元、英镑和瑞郎兑美元的涨幅分列前三。2019年内,市场风险事件频发,但美元意外彰显出来的避险价值,一度令其他传统避险货币表现逊色。不过随着临近年底时中美达成"第一阶段"

贸易协议，风险情绪大受提振，这令瑞郎从11月底的大跌1.86%反转成全年上涨1.4%。但整体受到中美贸易冲突的影响，人民币兑美元下挫了1.45%，而英镑受脱欧局势明朗的影响在年尾发力，兑美元大涨4.04%。同时加元则受到美墨加协议（USMCA）和油价的提振，兑美元全线急升4.74%，领涨于各主要货币对。

总体来看，2019年外汇市场属于趋势逆转紧迫、震荡风险加剧的局面。同时美联储迫于经济放缓忧虑而三次降息，但并未改变美元整体企稳的趋势。然而在新的一年里，由于诸多重磅事件都将一一揭晓，美国国内外的压力都指向美元贬值，因此央行政策依然将成为主要焦点，尤其是需要观察发达经济体和新兴市场的分歧。

2.1.1 美元指数：展现韧性　高位震荡

美元指数是衡量美元在国际外汇市场汇率变化的一项综合指标，由美元兑六个主要国际货币（欧元、日元、英镑、加元、瑞典克朗和瑞士法郎）的汇率经过加权几何平均数计算得出。

2019年美联储在前一年完成四次加息之后实施了三次降息，主要还是因为强势美元确实已经给美国经济增长带来隐患。在最新12月的政策会议上，美联储除了维持利率不变，还下调了对至2022年的利率预期。根据点阵图显示，官员们预期2020年将维持一年的按兵不动，之后两年或每年各加息一次。

美联储主席鲍威尔在之后的新闻发布会上也强调加息的条件是通胀水平显著且持续的上升。鲍威尔指出，美国经济前景仍令人满意，但经济现状不同于1998年，没有那么多的加息必要。

美银美林认为美联储12月决议释放了"长时期按兵不动"的立场，预期最早的调整将推迟至2021年下半年。

Action Economics机构首席经济学家Mike Englund也认为："美国经济在2019年收尾之际，GDP增长、产量增加、工时增加，较低通胀的表现都较年初预期的更好，这些因素很可能在2020年继续真实，市场对美国经济扩张的时间长度有所低估。"

图2.2　2019年美元指数走势图

美元指数2019年开于96.09,之后便维持震荡走高的态势,虽然年内涨幅并不显著,但考虑到美联储完成了三次降息,能够交出这样一份成绩单已经实属不易。深究原因,除了美联储的鹰派降息以外,主要还是其他经济体的相对表现糟糕,尤其是欧元区领头羊德国经济放缓迹象愈发明显,这令欧洲央行的宽松预期不断升温,从而帮助美元指数一度在10月1日触及年内高位的99.68,逼近100大关。另一方面,年内最大的风险来自中美贸易局势。通常在贸易冲突的情况下,美元的避险属性会受到投资者的追捧,这也为美元带来了许多避险买盘。

2.1.2 欧元/美元:内忧外患 稳步下跌

2019年受多方相互制约的因素影响,欧元/美元一直维持窄幅震荡,并有望创史上最窄年度波动区间。在最新的决议中,欧洲央行强调,将继续以每月200亿欧元的规模购债,QE将持续到首次加息以后。不过有一点值得注意:欧洲央行政策声明并未提到政策评估。鉴于欧元区经济在制造业萧条的背景下难以取得经济增长,欧洲央行已经允许对欧元区提供更多的政策支持,使得新任行长拉加德在考虑改变政策前拥有足够的时间和空间做决定。

欧元区面临与日俱增的债务风险,投资者追逐更高风险与收益资产的倾向在低利率环境中得到放大。尽管欧洲央行已准备好放宽信贷条件,但是如果经济状况恶化,其政策在短期提供的潜在刺激效果会否随时间推移而抵消将不得而知。

图2.3 2019年欧元/美元走势图

欧元/美元2019年开于1.146 5,之后便开启了稳步下跌的走势,并于10月1日触及年内低位1.087 7,跌至两年半新低,因德国当日公布的9月CPI表现不及预期,这进一步增加了欧洲央行宽松的预期。与此同时,德国主要经济研究机构也下调了对欧洲最大经济体德国的增长预期。但随着接近年底,英国有序脱欧概率逐步提升,不确定性下降有助于欧元区经济的复苏,从而帮助欧元能够收复部分失地。

2019年欧元走势的谨小慎微可以体现出欧元区年内面临的内忧外患,错综复杂的多重因素令欧元走势暂难破局,其中英国脱欧进程无疑是限制未来经济前景的关键因素之一。自2018年年初以来,欧元兑美元从未收于200日移动均线上方(目前大约在1.115 4附近),因此这里将成为欧元进入2020年后走势的关键枢纽。

2.1.3　美元/日元:避险需求高企　日元全年涨幅近1%

虽然2019年市场避险需求依然高企,但随着贸易情绪的好转,日元依然适度上涨近1%。

日本央行在最新的政策会议上继续按兵不动,并表示,如果风险加大,将毫不犹豫进一步放宽货币政策。然而市场分析师普遍认为,日本央行进一步扩大宽松政策的门槛实际上是非常高的。考虑到新一年中市场将迎来英国脱欧、中美贸易局势以及美国总统大选等一系列重磅事件的考验,传统避险资产日元应该不会缺乏买盘支撑。然而一旦全球局势趋稳,日本投资者对海外资产的需求以及企业并购活动重新抬头必然会限制日元的反弹空间。

图2.4　2019年美元/日元走势图

该货币对走势的大方向依然与中美贸易局势紧密相连,8月26日受到美方宣布将提高对约5 500亿美元中国输美商品加征关税税率的消息影响,该货币对一度跌至104.44的年内低位,并触及2016年11月来最低。之后随着中美贸易谈判出现了积极进展,风险情绪改观再度打压了日元的避险需求,从而令该货币对进入第四季度后稳步回升。

2.1.4　英镑/美元:惊心动魄的一年

2019年对于英镑而言可以说是惊心动魄的一年。英国脱欧遭遇多番挫折,甚至直接导致特蕾莎·梅下台。而约翰逊接任首相一职后,也经历了多次打击。无论是脱欧协议屡遭议会否决,还是提前大选一度搁浅,让英镑前三季度不断下探新低。受英国政治不确定性影响,英镑兑美元9月3日一度跌至1.195 7,达到2016年10月闪崩以来的最低。

不过,随着进入第四季度,约翰逊政府开始在脱欧问题上逐步掌握局势。在新版脱欧协议迟迟不能在议会得到通过后,约翰逊试图通过提前大选来提升掌控权。终于功夫不负有心人,在失败了

图2.5 2019年英镑/美元走势图

3次后，第4次"提前大选"动议在10月30日终获下议院通过，英国迎来近一个世纪以来首次12月大选。随着民调显示，保守党获胜概率不断攀升，英镑也开始强势反弹。最终在12月的大选中，约翰逊的保守党以压倒性的优势获胜，兑美元一度攻克1.35关口，涨幅达到2.5%，触及19个月高位的同时还录得20世纪90年代以来最大日线涨幅之一。

然而，谁也没想到的是，就在短短一周之后，英镑兑美元迅速回吐约翰逊赢得大选后的全部涨幅。一度暴跌超400点，兑美元创下逾三年最大单周跌幅，兑欧元也创下了自2017年7月以来的最大单周跌幅。

不过，随着约翰逊脱欧协议获得通过的概率日益攀升，以及美元避险需求的下降，英镑在12月底再度发力，最终兑美元全年大涨逾4%。

但考虑到约翰逊排除了延长脱欧过渡期的可能性，将与欧盟达成贸易协议的最后期限定在2020年12月，这导致硬脱欧疑虑卷土重来，市场依然担心双方届时若达不成协议，可能会迎来另一个英国脱欧的"断崖"。

2.1.5 澳元/美元：痛苦的一年 贬值压力攀升

2019年对于澳元而言又是痛苦的一年，在澳元最终由跌转涨后依然录得下跌。因其与中国经济的高度相关性，导致在全球经济偏向下行以及中美贸易不确定性存在的2019年中，澳洲联储不得不三次降息以缓解经济压力，这也令澳元贬值压力攀升。

10月1日，澳洲联储宣布下调基准利率25个基点至0.75%的历史新低，这是继6月、7月后的年内第3次降息。澳元兑美元短线跌破0.6700重要关口，触及年内低位0.6668。第三季度下跌3.8%，创造了2016年第四季度以来最大季度跌幅。虽然进入第四季度后，由于中美贸易谈判出现积极进展，以及"第一阶段"贸易协议的达成，帮助澳元重获反弹动能，但外汇交易员仍在卖出澳元，因预期澳洲联储到2020年将进一步放松货币政策。

图2.6　2019年澳元/美元走势图

2.1.6　美元/加元：贸易局势稳定提振加元

虽然早在2018年下旬，美国、墨西哥和加拿大已经就新版贸易协定达成一致，但由于美国民主党议员对其中一些条款有异议，协定一直迟迟无法获得正式批准。在经过新一轮谈判和修订后，三国代表终于在2019年12月11日正式签署了新版的美墨加协议（USMCA），现在只等三个国家各自的议会批准，这份协定就可开始实施。美墨加协议得到显著进展帮助稳定了北美贸易局势，也提振加元有效反弹。

图2.7　2019年美元/加元走势图

与此同时，油价的震荡走高以及加拿大央行态度的转变也帮助加元在2019年企稳。加拿大央行在5月政策会议上的鸽派态度一度令美元/加元急涨至1.356 4的1月来新高。但随着时间的推移和局势的变化,加拿大央行在整个2019年继续按兵不动,同时在接近年底时态度愈发显现鹰派。在12月的政策会议上,尽管加拿大央行表达了对与贸易冲突相关的担忧,但其对加拿大经济的韧性表示赞赏。总体而言,加拿大经济表现良好,央行不太可能在短期内降息。这种乐观情绪与美联储最近暂停降息的举动一致。

相信只要新版美墨加协议能够最终落实,贸易局势改善除了直接会提振加元以外,对油价的支撑也会变相进一步推高加元。这也是为什么2019年加元兑美元能够成为最大的赢家。

2.1.7 美元/人民币:"七"上"七"下

人民币兑美元破7无疑成为2019年的关注焦点。8月5日离岸、在岸人民币兑美元双双跌破7关口,日内跌幅一度超过1 000点。中国央行随后表示,受单边主义和贸易保护主义措施及对中国加征关税预期等影响,今日人民币对美元汇率有所贬值,突破了7元,但人民币对一篮子货币继续保持稳定和强势,这是市场供求和国际汇市波动的反映。

图2.8 2019年美元/人民币走势图

随着中美贸易局势的进展愈加乐观,人民币汇率也在第四季度开启了反弹之路。12月13日,中美双方证实达成"第一阶段"协议,并表态不会在12月15日开始加征新一轮关税。这令贸易局势获得了显著推动,虽然市场还在等待更具有实质性的签署落实,但市场情绪无疑已经出现了良好的转变。这也有助于人民币汇率企稳。同时一旦贸易局势趋稳,美元的避险价值将受到打压,将有利于人民币的进一步反弹。

尽管针对中美的第一阶段贸易协议,有分析指出,此次协议的达成是一个多赢的结果,不仅有利于缓和已经紧绷的中美关系,也实质性地有利于双方的经济利益,对世界经济与贸易的稳定发展也释放了正面消息。不过,与此同时也必须认识到,第一阶段协议还未最终尘埃落定,第二阶段谈判前景如何也未可知。

正如中国外交部副部长郑泽光在国新办新闻发布会上说的那样,中美第一阶段贸易协议的达成,有利于中国,有利于美国,有利于世界。经过建交40年的发展,中美利益深度交融,需要合作应对的全球性挑战越来越多,这也包括全球经济、金融的稳定和发展。40年中美关系给予人们最大的启示是:中美合则两利、斗则俱伤,合作是唯一正确的选择;相互尊重、求同存异才是中美两国的相处之道。

2.2 2019年主要货币对波动率分析

一般投资者理解的波动率是计算价格或收益率的标准方差进行比较，样本标准差都是衡量一个样本波动大小的量，样本标准差越大，样本数据的波动就越大。即使两组数据的平均值相同，也可能会得出不同的标准方差，其中标准方差较大的一组数据说明个体之间的波动较大。

本书选取2019年各个主要货币对的全年日收盘价计算得出的标准方差作为波动率参考，结合全年涨跌幅进行投资比较。其中，美元指数全年上涨0.44%，波动率为0.824 5，远小于2018年；欧元/美元全年下跌2.22%，波动率为0.013 5，在2018年基础上继续减小；美元/日元全年下跌0.96%，波动率为1.585 4，小于2018年；英镑/美元全年上涨4.04%，波动率为0.033 3，小于2018年；澳元/美元全年下跌0.45%，波动率为0.014 4，小于2018年；美元/加元全年下挫4.74%，波动率为0.012，远小于2018年；美元/离岸人民币全年上涨1.45%，波动率为0.146 6，远小于2018年。

通过数据比较可以看出，2019年外汇市场整体展现出波幅缩小的现象。无论是哪个货币对均小于2018年的波动幅度，表明在错综复杂的局势下，投资者更加克制。其中最具代表性的是欧元/美元，该货币对2019年一直维持窄幅震荡，并创史上最窄年度波动区间。作为所有货币对中流动性最高者，欧元/美元是交易商可以赚钱的最安全投资之一，对于任何投资于利差交易的人来说，低波动性都是一个绿灯，因为汇率损失的风险极小。

2 全球货币市场篇

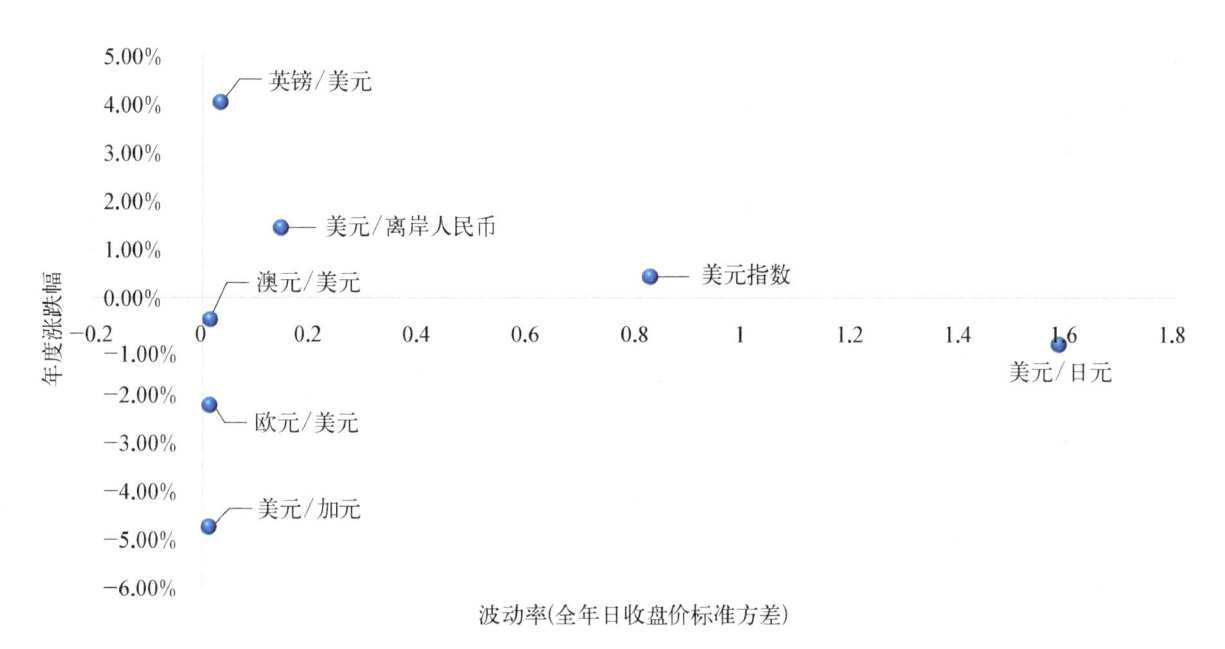

图2.9 2019年主要货币涨跌和波动率表现

2.3 2020年全球货币市场展望

虽然美联储已经表态,降息已经按下"暂停键",然而,人们越来越期待中美贸易战将得到解决,这在2019年年底的时候导致全球股市持续走高,而美元也回吐了部分涨幅,导致许多市场人士质疑美元的涨势是否即将结束。自2018年以来,美元一直在攀升。然而,与投资者乐观情绪同时出现的是,最近几周涨势看似已经见顶。美元涨势见顶之际,市场对中美两国将签署"第一阶段"协议的预期近来也在升温。高盛经济学家预计,全球经济增长将在2020年有所复苏,这将为美元在国际市场上走软创造环境。眼下市场普遍认为强势美元大概率会在新的一年面临打击,因此投资者应当适时地减少美元多头押注。这主要是出于四个理由。

第一,美国总统特朗普已经多次施压美联储,虽然美联储反复强调政策的独立性,但如果贸易局势压力增加,以及特朗普大选支持率攀升的话,美联储对货币政策控制权或许会降低,这无疑增加了美元的下行空间。

第二,中美贸易局势虽然还面临一系列问题的挑战,但无论是中国还是美国,对达成协议的意愿还是很强烈的,这也是对双方都有好处的。而贸易争端在2019年一直成为美元避险买盘的一个重要支撑。

第三,随着各国的宽松加码,2020年全球经济有望获得除财政刺激手段以外更大的助力,2019年这种美国经济一枝独秀的局面恐难再现,这也会压缩美元的相对强势表现空间。

第四,鉴于各国货币政策工具箱的捉襟见肘,相信更多央行对于去美元化的需求正在攀升,这也会减弱新一年美元的政府买盘。

在美元走弱的主流预期下,目前认为相对而言最为安全的汇市操作选择无疑是做空美元/日元,巴克莱分析师就曾指出,2019年秋季以来美元/日元转为上行,主要是受到中美贸易紧张局势缓解以及英国脱欧风险降低的影响,但空头需要有些耐心,因为我们认为随着全球经济周期的反弹,该货币对在2020年上半年依然会受到稳固支撑。同时日本投资者对海外资产的需求以及企业并购活动的增加,这也将帮助该货币对企稳。然而全球经济复苏速度的放缓还是会限制该货币对的上行空间。此外,我们发现日本央行进一步扩大宽松政策的概率也在降低。高盛方面同样认为,美元/日元短线料将涨向110关口,中期内则预计做空该货币对仍然是对冲全球衰退风险的最佳选择。进入新一年后,巴克莱分析师预测美元/日元在2020年上半年料将受到108一线的有效支撑,但在下半年将因美国大选而跌至105附近。整体来看,日元可以为投资者在2020年资产配置中提供安全保障,因此是一个对冲风险的不错选择。

其他主要货币方面,各大主要机构普遍认为欧元在经历了压抑的一年后应该会在2020年大放异彩。2019年受多方相互制约的因素影响,欧元/美元一直维持窄幅震荡,并有望创史上最窄年度波动区间。作为所有货币对中流动性最高者,欧元/美元是交易商可以赚钱的最安全投资之一,对于任何投资于利差交易的人来说,低波动性都是一个绿灯,因为汇率损失的风险极小。同时随着新一年贸易局势的逐渐明朗,英国有序脱欧的概率攀升,相信欧元做多操作有望获得不错的回报。首先,根据高盛模型显示,欧元被低估了15%。这种低估在很大程度上是由欧元区继续保持国际收支盈余推动的。其次,全球外汇市场的参与者已经大量做空欧元,高盛数据显示:"过去一年,杠杆基金每周做空欧元/美元的头寸至少达100亿美元。"当市场大量押注于单向时,随着押注的结束,出现大幅而有意义逆转的可能性会增大。第三,欧洲央行的利率似乎无法远低于当前水平。(外汇市场的经验法则是,当一家央行降低利率时,它发行的货币就会贬值。因此,欧洲央行已经触底的利率不再拖累欧元)。

2.3.1 2020年汇市四大潜在"黑天鹅"需要密切关注

- **英国硬脱欧风险意外上升**

虽然保守党大胜增加了约翰逊对脱欧形势的掌控,同时英国下议院议员们以358票对234票的结果通过了约翰逊政府的脱欧协议法案,这意味着,英国将结束持续3年多的不确定性,于2020年1月31日脱离欧盟。新的脱欧协议法案还明确了脱欧过渡期不能推迟至2020年12月31日之后,这进一步加大了英国无协议脱欧的风险,因英国要在不到一年的时间内和欧盟达成一份满意的贸易协议并非易事。

- **特朗普选情回暖,但若失利可能搅乱市场**

和2016年一样,现任美国总统的支持者多为老年白人,但"千禧一代"逐渐成熟并掌握话语权,这样的情况显然不乐观。"千禧一代",或者年纪更大一点的选民,更能感受到气候变化与美国收入分配中的不平等,而现任美国总统却主导退出巴黎气候协定以及对大公司减税。一旦特朗普失利,许多现行政策恐将面临冲击。同时,虽然是特朗普一手挑起的贸易战,但民主党人士对中国的态度实际上可能更差,若民主党上台,未来的中美贸易谈判将会何去何从还不得而知,但可以肯定的是,不确定性无疑会大幅攀升。

- **匈牙利退出欧盟**

匈牙利自2004年加入欧盟以来,在经济上取得了令人瞩目的成功。但在欧盟启动针对匈牙利的第7条款后,长达15年的联盟关系似乎陷入了麻烦。欧盟不满匈牙利的理由是匈牙利的国内政策不符合欧盟价值观,因此不排除匈牙利在2020年底前跟随英国脱离欧盟。这可能会进一步打乱欧元区一体化的布局,从而令欧洲局势更加扑朔迷离。

- **亚投行发行数字货币**

美元作为世界主要储备货币,无论是对美国,还是对其他国家来说,都始终是一把双刃剑。其他国家通过美元吸收全球资本,推动经济增长。但弊端也显而易见,每当美国与任何一个国家发生不愉快,美元就会变成一个致命的威胁。亚洲投行创建了一种新的储备资产,称为ADR(Asian Drawing Right,亚洲提款权),即1个ADR相当于2美元,使ADR成为世界上最大的货币单位。ADR是由区块链技术驱动的,被该地区的中央银行视为储备货币,与黄金储备、当前非美元外汇储备等资产相当的一种资产。作为储备资产,ADR不可向公众交易,但它代表一篮子货币和黄金,其中人民币在组合中占据重要地位,美元权重低于20%。相信若果真推出,可能会加速美元的贬值。

2.3.2 具备升值趋势的货币:欧元、英镑

- **欧元**

随着美国经济增速放缓,欧元区经济增长有望回升,这将对欧元提供反弹动能。欧元区经济表现的改善,可能会转化为欧元区主权债务特别是德国主权债务的债券收益率上升,这反过来将对欧元形成支持。

近期的数据显示,欧元区经济尤其是德国经济可能已经见底,并可能在2020年开始逐步回升。欧元区第三季度GDP年率修正值增长1.2%,好于此前预期增长1.1%。

欧洲央行行长拉加德在上任后似乎将重点放在加大财政刺激的必要性上,以应对欧元区的增长和通胀问题。这令市场降低对欧洲央行降息的预期,有利于欧元前景。

此外,随着贸易紧张局势的缓解和英国脱欧不确定性的降低,政治因素也将对欧元形成正面支撑。

事实上,越来越多的投行以及机构分析师看好2020年欧元前景(见表2.1):

表2.1 机构对2020年欧元前景的展望

投行名称	观点	关键点位
摩根士丹利(看多欧元)	2020年做多欧元/美元,欧美经济增长差异正在缩小,股市资金流动以及政治局势也在变化。	预计到2020年3月底,欧元/美元升至1.16,到2020年6月底将进一步涨至1.18。
加拿大帝国商业银行(看多欧元)	放眼2020年,继续相信欧元将会逐步升值。	预计2020年第一季度欧元/美元将涨至1.12,第三季度将涨至1.15。
高盛(看多欧元)	欧元/美元将在2020年后期回升,有三个关键因素将共同推动欧元走强,首先,根据高盛模型,欧元被低估15%。其次,全球外汇市场的参与者已经大量做空欧元。第三,欧洲央行的利率似乎无法远低于当前水平。	预计欧元/美元将在12个月内反弹至1.15。
大华银行(看多欧元)	欧元/美元预计将在明年强势走高。	预计到2020年底欧元/美元将升至1.1500。

(续表)

投 行 名 称	观　　　点	关 键 点 位
投资管理公司Insight Investment（看多欧元）	欧元区经济接近拐点。从目前的前景看，形势将缓慢好转，欧元值得长期持有。	2020年欧元/美元可能上涨至1.15。
瑞银（看多欧元）	预计美元在2020年下跌，因此欧元/美元将大幅上涨。	2020年底欧元/美元料达到1.19。
荷兰国际银行（看空欧元）	由于欧元区基本面疲弱，想投机欧元/美元仍然没有吸引力，回报潜力有限。	预计2020年欧元/美元在1.10—1.15区间波动，下行风险明显。

- 英镑

因英国保守党以压倒性优势赢得提前大选，令市场憧憬英国将顺利脱欧，英镑汇率自9月初以来出现大涨。展望2020年，英镑走势主要将受到英国脱欧、英国经济基本面以及英国央行利率走向等因素的驱动。

随着英国首相约翰逊在大选中大获全胜，英国很有可能通过立法以在2020年1月31日脱欧。英欧关系随后进入过渡期，暂时维持现状，以便双方就脱欧后全面贸易关系达成协议。过渡期定于2020年12月31日结束。

英国首相约翰逊表示，一旦确认2020年1月31日英国脱欧，将会否决任何延长过渡期的建议。因此，一旦英国和欧盟未能在年底前完成贸易谈判，英国仍将硬脱欧，这对于英镑走势不利。

假如英国能够避免硬脱欧，那么英镑可能更多受到经济基本面的推动。市场人士乐观地认为，英国经济在最近几个月停滞后，将在2020年实现反弹，这将进一步提振英镑。

至于2020年英国央行利率前景，目前市场存在分歧，认为英国央行存在降息或者加息的可能性。因此，英国通胀数据至关重要。持续疲软的通胀可能导致英国央行在2020年年中降息；但假如英国通胀持续高于央行设定的2%目标，则加息压力将加大，这将推高英镑。

整体来看，虽然英镑近期的大幅回调令未来前景蒙上阴影，但多数机构依然是乐观地看多英镑，尤其是在更长周期内。澳洲国民银行分析师表示："英镑已经回吐了大选获胜后的涨幅，未来一年内预计将会较为波动，但考虑到工党的威胁已经消除了，英镑表现应该会比之前的表现更好。"

分析师预计无协议脱欧的概率小于10%，这令英镑长期走势看涨，但短期内风险依然存在。然而英镑/美元的下行空间料将受限于1.277 5，欧元/英镑的涨幅则将受阻于0.872 5。随着接近2020年底时，脱离WTO的选项被避免后，英镑有望兑美元和欧元分别回升至1.40和0.83。

2.3.3　表现相对平稳的货币：澳元、日元

- 澳元

澳元和纽元对中国的敏感性都较高，主要是受到紧密的贸易关系的影响。不过随着中国经济数据逐步企稳，同时中美贸易谈判出现积极进展，相信在新一年中，"第一阶段"协议的签署将会帮助澳元和纽元保持反弹。多伦多道明银行（TD）分析师表示："全球经济增长前景依然是澳元最大的驱动因素之一。投资情绪受到中美贸易关系的影响，已经对澳元等敏感性货币造成压力。然而，过去十年内，澳元已经建立了健康的外部平衡，尤其是经常账的表现。同时资金流动的变化也表明

澳元目前被严重低估,大约较公允值被低估了10%。因此随着负面因素的减弱,以及全球经济增长的稳步复苏,相信澳元将逐步收复这些被低估区域。"

不过,需要注意的是,考虑到经济前景,市场普遍预期澳洲联储可能在2020年降息两次。澳洲联储也在最新的政策会议上表示,鉴于降息的滞后性,准备好在必要时放宽货币政策。预计利率将在较长一段时间处于低位是合理的。澳洲国民银行(NAB)曾发布报告指出,中期支撑和阻力水平看来旗鼓相当,预计澳元/美元将在未来数周内整体维持在0.67—0.69交投区间。只有突破这一区间才能为中期走势提供指引。高盛预计澳元/美元在12个月后料报0.70。

- 日元

在美元走弱的主流预期下,目前认为相对而言最为安全的汇市操作选择无疑是做空美元/日元,巴克莱分析师就曾指出,2019年秋季以来美元/日元转为上行,主要是受到中美贸易紧张局势缓解以及英国脱欧风险降低的影响,但空头需要有些耐心,因为该行认为随着全球经济周期的反弹,该货币对在2020年上半年依然会受到稳固支撑。

同时,日本投资者对海外资产的需求以及企业并购活动的增加,也将帮助该货币对企稳。然而全球经济复苏速度的放缓还是会限制该货币对的上行空间。此外,还发现日本央行进一步扩大宽松政策的概率也在降低。

高盛方面则同样认为,美元/日元短线料将涨向110关口,中期内则预计做空该货币对仍然是对冲全球衰退风险的最佳选择。进入新一年后,巴克莱分析师预测美元/日元2020年上半年料将受到108一线的有效支撑,但在下半年将因美国大选而跌至105附近。整体来看,日元在2020年做多的获利空间可能不大,但可以为投资者在2020年资产配置中提供更加安全的保障,因此是一个对冲风险的不错选择。

2.3.4 具有贬值趋势的货币:美元、加元

- 美元

美元确实顶住了2019年三次降息的冲击,昂首踏向新的一年。但本书中已经多次提到,美元其实面临着严重的内忧外患。美国政府倾向于美元走软,鉴于2020年美国可能会举行一场有争议的总统大选,2020年对看涨者来说可能是不稳定的一年,而这应该会继续支撑黄金,尤其是在地缘政治风险整体上占据上风的情况下。从技术上讲,多头正在2019年11月至2020年迄今的跌势的61.8%斐波那契回档位触顶,在200日均线附近形成一个强大的汇合阻力点。美元自6月底以来形成了上升楔形,这一图形在10月初达到顶点,眼下美元正处于下跌盘整中。

加拿大帝国商业银行(CIBC)分析师团队预测称,美元指数在未来几个季度将继续走低,2020年第一季美元指数料将交投于95.5,2020年第三季将降至93.4。该行指出,尽管美联储采取了一定程度的降息措施,而且保护主义没有解决不利的经常账户平衡问题,但美元在过去一年里还是成功反弹。在第四季度的增长步伐似乎有所放缓之后,由于利息敏感需求(尤其是住房)的改善,美国似乎有望在2020年初恢复增长。这应该会让美联储永远放弃降息工具,将对美元形成支撑。但该行认为,未来一年全球不确定性的逐步减少将抵消这一影响,这将导致美元的避险需求出现部分逆转。

此外,进入新的一年,美中贸易协定有待检验,英国脱欧后的贸易谈判仍存在不确定性,海外经

图2.10　2019年美元指数走势图

济疲软的迹象依然明显。较早出台的货币刺激措施的滞后影响,随着时间的推移,一些贸易文件的透明度,以及日本的财政刺激措施(未来可能还会出现在欧洲),可能会让世界在2020年末,在海外的基调有所改善。这种冒险的环境应该会让欧元和英镑复苏,而欧洲和日本优越的经常账户余额也应该有利于本币兑美元汇率。

- **加元**

虽然新版美墨加协议(USMCA)已经在年底完成签署,但未来还需要等待三国议会的批准,因此不能完全排除不确定性。另一方面,即便最终如期通过,加元实际上已经消化了美墨加协议带来的利好,因此更大的风险偏向下行。

更令人担心的是,最新数据显示加拿大10月经济意外萎缩0.1%,这令加拿大经济的疲软前景再度加强,从而可能会提升加拿大央行的降息概率。加拿大帝国商业银行(CIBC)发布报告指出:"我们预期美元/加元短线将会维持区间震荡。尽管如此,放眼2020年第一季度,我们预期加拿大国内的基本面情况以及全球增长面的疲软倾向将令加拿大央行降息25个基点。考虑到这样的局面并未被市场消化,因此可能会令加元适度走弱,预计美元/加元在2020年第一和第二季度将分别涨向1.33和1.34。"

同时分析师认为,长期而言,加元的走弱将会支撑加拿大经常账和贸易账表现。更值得注意的是,加元贬值将会帮助加拿大对美国出口重新复苏,因此预计美元/加元在2020年第四季度涨向1.38附近,同时2021年有望进一步上看1.40大关。

尽管如此,市场还是需要关注原油市场的表现。在第17届OPEC与非OPEC产油国部长级监督委员会(JMMC)会议上,双方已经就扩大减产达成一致,在2020年第一季度双方将合理额外减产50万桶/日,从而令减产规模扩大至170万桶/日。170万桶/日相当于全球原油总需求的1.7%,同时更值得注意的是,沙特能源大臣阿卜杜勒-阿齐兹随后表示,额外减产中沙特将承担16.7万桶/日,同时还将继续自愿减产40万桶/日,指出只要减产执行率得到改善,OPEC+的有效减产规模将高达210万桶/日。原油价格若能稳步走高,相信会为加元提供一定支撑。但值得注意的是,近年来油价对加元的影响力正在下降,主要是因为贸易和经济前景成为市场的主导因素。

2.3.5 具有崩盘风险的货币：南非兰特

- **南非兰特**

谈及2019年最惨的货币，毫无疑问不少人都会想到阿根廷比索。2019年8月11日的阿根廷总统初选大爆冷门，现任总统被对手击败，引爆阿根廷股市盘中重挫37%，阿根廷比索汇率盘中重挫33%，债市盘中重挫20%。比索兑美元盘中生挫33%，当日便创下60比索兑换1美元的历史新低。随着阿根廷债务违约危机的恶化以及该国经济前景的暗淡，比索还在不断地创造历史新低。考虑到国际货币基金组织（IMF）的介入，以及该国的货币管制措施，相信新一年继续崩盘的概率将有所下降。

但如果对阿根廷债务的担忧不断加剧，结合南非自身疲软的经济增长，南非兰特或成为土耳其里拉、阿根廷比索之后，2020年具有崩盘风险的货币。

据南非独立传媒网站2019年11月15日报道，评级机构穆迪将南非2020年经济增长预期从1.5%下调至1%，称全球因素正在对新兴经济体产生影响。穆迪表示，尽管有迹象表明南非的货币政策方向正在收紧，但贸易紧张局势和地缘政治风险已带来了额外的不确定性，使长期支出和投资决策变得困难。预计南非经济在2021年仅增长1.2%。

分析师指出，因投资者对南非经济前景感到担忧，目前南非兰特正遭到抛售。因此，虽然南非兰特一度出现过复苏迹象，但基本面问题若不能解决，结合外部不利因素的发酵，相信2020年对于南非兰特而言还是险象环生的。

3

国际黄金市场篇

3.1 2019年黄金市场回顾：美降息等多因素叠加 金价快速上行

3.1.1 黄金的基础属性解析

中国古语说："盛世藏古董，乱世买黄金。"黄金从来都不是一种简单的商品，而是一种具有商品属性、货币属性和投资属性的稀有商品。

从商品属性的角度来说，黄金可以用来日常消费和工业加工，可以做成首饰、工艺品，也可以作为工业生产原料、化学化工原料等。

货币属性上，马克思说过："金银天然不是货币，但货币天然是金银。"自从人类开始社会分工出现交易需要之后，黄金和白银就成为很多商品经济比较发达的国家交换的中介，黄金作为货币的属性在货币史上是跟随着货币的改革同步进行的。在金银本位制和金本位制下，黄金一直都是流通中货币的基础，也是支付的基础货币。后期的金融制度改革的基础并不是因为黄金不适合作为最终支付手段，而是随着工业革命的发展，商品贸易极大丰富，而黄金数量相对有限，这种状况下黄金无法应对全球规模如此大的商贸活动。因此，后期出现过银行券+黄金本位制，布雷顿体系下的美元+黄金本位制，而这些货币体系后面的最终支付手段还是基于黄金，但是又不完全依靠黄金。而在布雷顿森林体系崩溃后，国际货币体系进入牙买加体系下的浮动汇率制度，黄金不再作为最后的支付手段，其货币化地位被弱化。虽然黄金已经不成为货币体系的最后支付手段，但是各国央行依旧在大量储备黄金，而结算中黄金也可以用来进行结算，因此黄金虽然不作为最后的支付手段，但是依旧保留其部分的货币属性。

从投资属性来说，黄金长久以来一直都是资产的代表，是一种重要的财富储藏手段。传统的投资方式主要是买实物黄金，比如金条、金块等,现在黄金作为投资品选择范围就非常宽泛了,如黄金ETF、纸黄金、黄金期货、黄金现货等。当前黄金的货币属性已经大大减弱,而其资产属性就成为当前投资的重要影响因素。

黄金的多重属性造成黄金在定价上比一般的投资品更加复杂,在不同的经济周期和阶段,影响黄金价格的因素会有比较大的变化。因此在黄金投资上,需要把黄金投资的多种影响因素放在一个框架下进行分析和思考。

3.1.2　2019年度黄金价格走势分析

截止到2019年12月31日,国际现货黄金价格已经从1 282.07美元/盎司上涨到1 520.17美元/盎司,上涨幅度为18.57%。对黄金的分析一般来说可以从供需、抵御通胀和避险三个角度来进行。2019年度整体来说供需上没有出现比较大的变化,唯一有亮点的是各国央行对黄金的增持。2019年度对黄金影响更直接的因素是美元利率下降和年度风险事件不断。从利率角度来说,从八月份开始美国利率政策开始进入降息通道,截止到2019年10月31日,联邦利率已经从2.25%—2.5%的区间降至1.5%—1.75%区间,利率的下降对黄金上涨形成比较强的支撑。避险方面,2019年中美贸易战成为全球经济不确定性中最大的影响因素,其他比较大的事件包括美国与伊朗之间的地缘政治紧张,围绕英国退欧引起的英国与欧洲的各种政治经济的不确定。

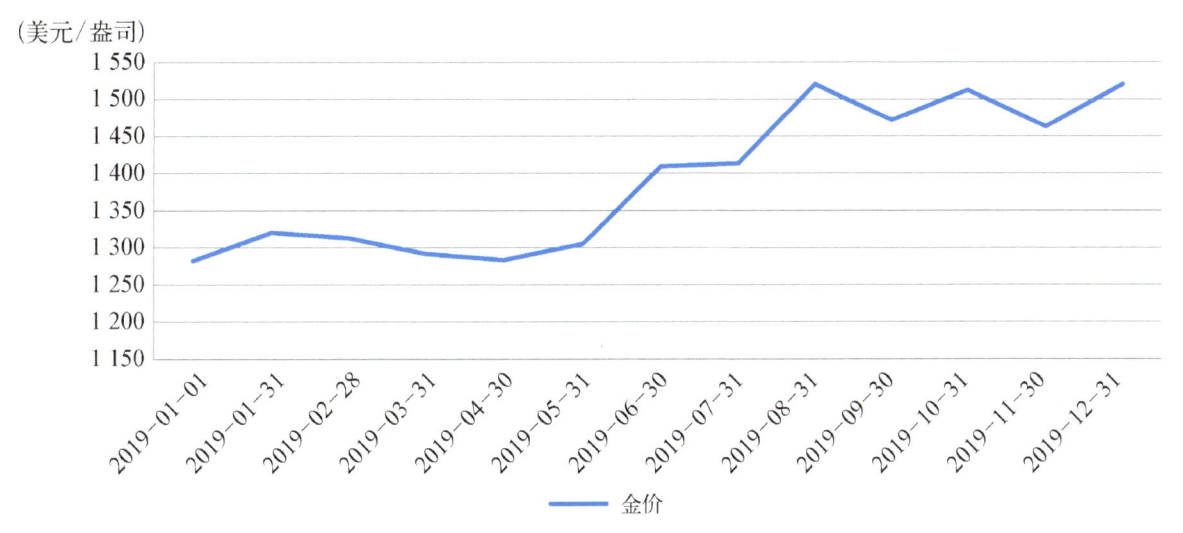

数据来源:FX168财经网。

图3.1　2019年黄金价格

对黄金投资的分析主要是对黄金基于其三大属性延伸出来的功能的分析,因此黄金分析要参考以下几个重要的指标:全球黄金的供需状况;基于通胀的保值因素;避险因素。

（1）全球黄金供需对黄金价格的影响

黄金的商品属性虽然对黄金价格影响并不是很大,但是黄金本身作为一种稀有金属,存量很少,而且开采成本较高。截至2018年年底,已经开采出来的黄金约为19.3万吨,其中大约9.2万吨用于珠宝首饰,4.1万吨用于私人投资,3.3万吨用于各国央行的黄金储备,工业和化工原料用量为2.7万吨。目前已经探明未开采的黄金为5.4万吨。

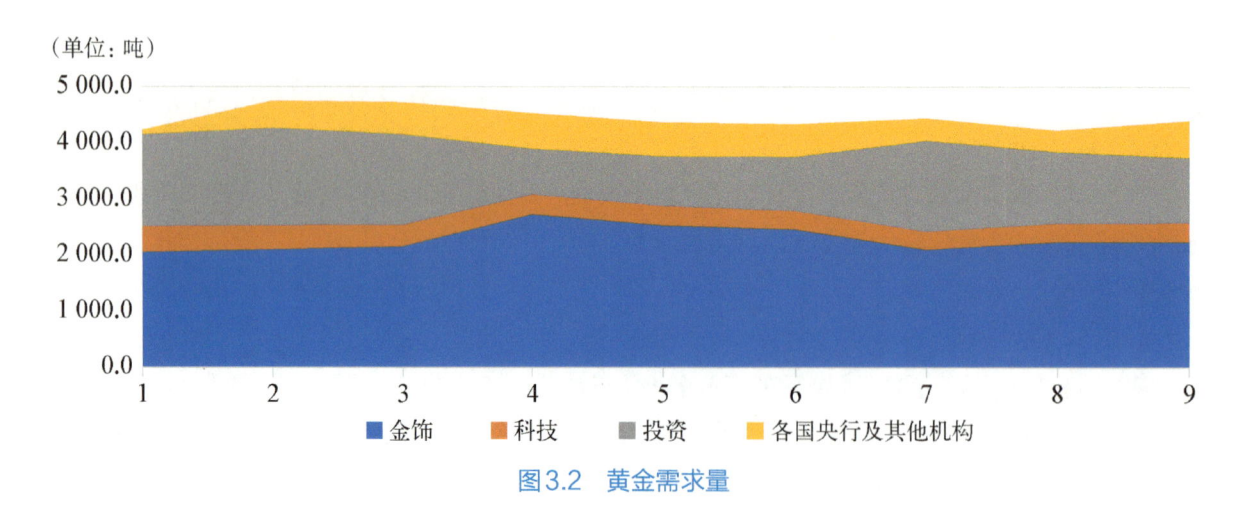

(单位：吨)

图3.2 黄金需求量

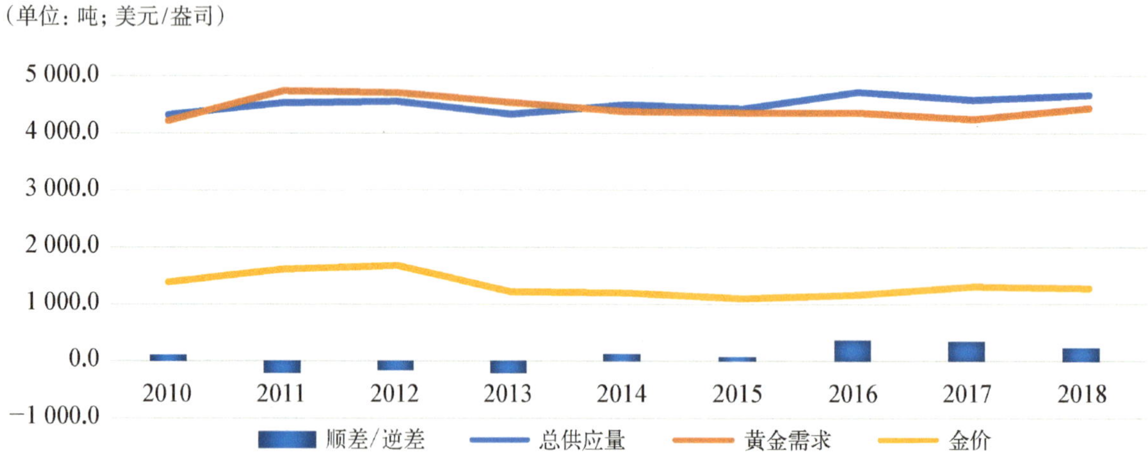

(单位：吨；美元/盎司)

数据来源：世界黄金协会。

图3.3 供需与价格

表3.1 2011年至2018年国际黄金市场供需状况   单位：吨

年　份	2011	2012	2013	2014	2015	2016	2017	2018
供应量	4 531.4	4 555.1	4 331.4	4 496.7	4 425.4	4 717.8	4 578.0	4 665.2
金矿产量	2 857.8	2 929.6	3 111.6	3 203.9	3 291.2	3 398.6	3 447.5	3 500.9
生产商净对冲额	22.5	−45.3	−27.9	104.9	12.9	37.6	−25.5	−12.5
再生金量	1 651.1	1 670.8	1 247.7	1 187.8	1 121.4	1 281.5	1 156.1	1 176.8
需求量	4 739.7	4 708.4	4 539.0	4 380.0	4 356.7	4 357.2	4 242.2	4 436.7
金　饰	2 092.1	2 141.2	2 736.0	2 543.3	2 478.2	2 017.4	2 255.1	2 281.7
科　技	429.1	382.3	355.8	348.4	331.7	323.0	332.6	334.8

(续表)

年份	2011	2012	2013	2014	2015	2016	2017	2018
加工量小计	2 521.3	2 523.5	3 091.8	2 891.7	2 809.9	2 340.4	2 587.7	2 616.4
金条和金币总需求量	1 502.3	1 311.7	1 730.4	1 066.1	1 090.8	1 072.2	1 046.0	1 091.7
黄金ETF及类似产品	235.4	304.0	−912.6	−178.9	−123.5	549.7	229.9	72.3
各国央行和其他机构	480.8	569.2	629.5	601.1	579.6	394.9	378.6	656.3
顺差/逆差	−208.3	−153.2	−207.6	116.7	68.7	360.6	335.8	228.5

数据来源：世界黄金协会。

从供需的角度来说，黄金的供给量在2010年到2012年间是需求大于供给，出现了供需上的黄金交叉，并且在2011年出现了近十年来黄金供需之间最大的逆差，需求比供给多出来208.3吨，而金价也在此阶段走出一波比较大的上涨行情，甚至在2011年9月6日创出历史新高1 920.6美元/盎司。因此黄金虽然在属性上来说，目前它的商品属性是一个比较弱的属性，但是依旧受到供需影响商品价格这个经济底层逻辑的影响。因此，在对未来黄金进行预测的时候，供需因素也是一个必须考量的因素。

表3.2　2017年第4季度至2019年第3季度国际黄金市场供需状况　　单位：吨

时间	2017年第4季度	2018年第1季度	2018年第2季度	2018年第3季度	2018年第4季度	2019年第1季度	2019年第2季度	2019年第3季度
供应量	1 163.0	1 156.0	1 122.9	1 179.7	1 206.6	1 135.5	1 227.0	1 222.3
金矿产量	898.0	842.7	869.2	883.3	905.8	844.2	861.3	877.8
生产商净对冲额	−9.3	37.5	−37.7	−24.1	11.8	−1.5	49.0	−9.2
再生金量	274.4	275.8	291.4	320.6	289.0	292.8	316.7	353.7
需求量	1 099.2	984.3	1 051.1	1 122.1	1 279.2	1 075.3	1 165.7	1 126.9
金饰	622.1	528.7	532.6	589.3	631.1	537.8	553.7	479.9
科技	88.3	81.8	83.3	85.4	84.3	80.0	81.0	82.2
加工量小计	710.4	610.5	615.9	674.6	715.4	617.8	634.6	562.1

(续表)

时间	2017年第4季度	2018年第1季度	2018年第2季度	2018年第3季度	2018年第4季度	2019年第1季度	2019年第2季度	2019年第3季度
金条和金币总需求量	259.5	261.3	248.2	298.2	284.1	258.3	220.1	150.3
黄金ETF及类似产品	35.7	27.7	34.2	−103.8	114.1	42.2	76.7	258.2
各国央行和其他机构	93.7	84.8	152.8	253.1	165.6	157.0	234.3	156.2
顺差/逆差	63.8	171.7	71.8	57.6	−72.7	60.3	61.3	95.4

数据来源：世界黄金协会。

从季度数据来看，2019年黄金供应量前三个季度都超过需求量，所以在2019年黄金市场的上涨并不是需求推动型上涨。从2017年四季度开始至2019年三季度，黄金的每季度需求量基本在984.3至1 227.00吨之间，从类型来说，金饰、工业用金和金条金币为主要使用方向，但其需求量相对来说是比较稳定的。ETF及类似产品由于跟随金价，所以需求量相对来说波动较大。另一个需求量比较大的来源是各国央行及其他机构，近几个季度需求量都比较大，季度需求都在150吨以上，是目前市场供需结构中比较大的影响点。因此供需结构上虽然现在不是决定黄金价格的关键因素，但是我们在进行黄金分析的时候，供需结构中的央行及其他机构的动作是我们要重点注意的一个参考因素。

（2）通货膨胀和利率对黄金价格的影响

黄金的另一个重要属性是它的投资属性，而在投资属性中，除了黄金是一个特殊的稀有金属外，主要由于黄金优秀的保值作用，它是抵御通货膨胀的重要资产。下面我们在全球通货膨胀的框架下对黄金进行分析。

由于国际黄金价格一般以美元进行标价，所以我们比较美国历史的通货膨胀数据，以通过数据关系寻找黄金与美国通货膨胀之间的关系。

我们通过对2010年到2018年美国CPI数据和黄金的走势比较可以看到，大的方面CPI和黄金价格是有一定的关联关系的，随着CPI的上涨，黄金价格会随之上涨，而随着CPI的下降，黄金价格也会随之下降。为了更好地表现这个问题，我们把当前的年度周期改成月度周期去比较这个数据。

另一个表现黄金价格保值作用的指标是美国实际利率水平，一般来说，黄金的价格和美国实际利率高度负相关。当美国利率上升的时候，代表可以产生利息的资产的收益率提高，这个时候相对来说不能产生利息的黄金价格就会收到抑制，同时当美元利率下降的时候，代表货币类资产价格开始走低，这个时候黄金的投资吸引力就会上升，从而推动黄金价格走高。

美国从2019年8月份开始进入降息周期，利息从2.25%—2.5%区间，经过三次降息已经降到

数据来源：FX168财经月历。

图3.4 CPI与黄金价格

1.5%—1.75%区间，在这个过程中，2019年度黄金价格出现大幅上涨，未来利率下调预期是支撑黄金价格进一步上涨的重要支撑力量。

数据来源：FX168财经月历。

图3.5 利率与黄金价格

（3）避险因素对黄金价格的影响

分析黄金走势的另一个主要维度是黄金的避险作用。所谓的"乱世买黄金"中的"乱世"，说的就是全球各类风险事件。历史上几乎每一次全球性的风险因素出现都会推动黄金价格的上涨。

2019年度在分析影响黄金的三个维度中，避险因素可能成为影响黄金价格涨跌的长期因素。当前全球经济进入严重的不确定性中，中美贸易战及未来围绕中美之间的战略博弈将会是全球经济和地缘政治中长期的不确定因素，美元利率倒挂，全球贸易规模收缩，更大方面基于全球贫富差距进一步拉大引起的全球动荡可能在短期内不会缓解，因此，我们有理由相信未来这些不确定性将会对黄金价格形成长期支撑。

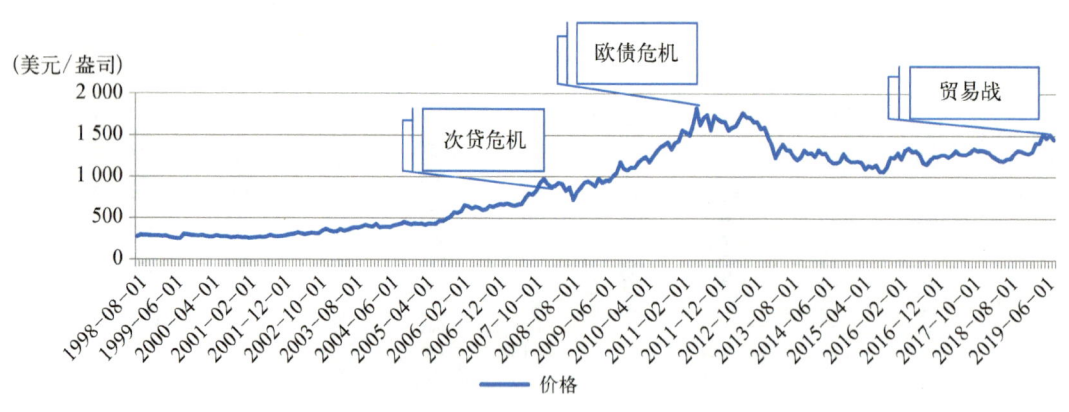

图3.6　风险因素与黄金价格

5.3 欧洲地区

5.3.1 英国：住房市场正在急剧放缓

英国的房价仍在上涨，尽管未按通胀因素调整。根据Nationwide的数据，截至2019年第三季度，英国平均房价小幅上涨0.33%（但经通胀因素调整后实际上下降了1.44%），至216 805英镑（276 968美元）。实际上，这是自2013年第一季度以来的最低同比增长。实际房价在上一季度几乎保持不变。

伦敦是截至2019年第三季度表现最差的地区，房价下跌1.7%（经通胀调整后为−3.4%），其次是大都市区（−1.5）和东南部地区（−0.6%）。伦敦的一些高端地区价格大幅下跌。

英国皇家特许测量师学会（RICS）称，英国住房市场可能将处于"停滞状态"，但长期的住房短缺将阻止价格大幅下跌。预计2019年房地产交易将比上年同期下降约5%，这主要是由于英国退欧公投的政治和经济不确定性，买家采取了更为谨慎的立场。

2019年第三季度，英国经济较上年同期增长了微不足道的1%。根据英国国家统计局（ONS）的数据，2019年第二季度同比增长1.3%。实际上，这是近十年来最低的同比增长。但是，经济避免了技术性衰退。英格兰银行将其对2019年经济增长的预测从先前的预测下调至1.3%。在2018年8月将英格兰银行（BoE）的关键利率提高25个基点之后，英格兰银行（BoE）的关键利率保持不变，仍为0.75%。

【英国伦敦房产数据】

表5.56 主要指标

价格收入比	22.02
抵押贷款占收入的百分比	150.52%
贷款承受能力指数	0.66
市中心租金价格比	34.64
出租价格比——中心以外	27.36
总租金收益率（市中心）	2.89%
总租金收益率（中心以外）	3.65%

表5.57 每月租金　　　　　　　　　　　　　　　单位：英镑

	每月租金均价	租金范围
市中心公寓（1间卧室）	1 696.86	1 250—2 250
市中心以外公寓（1间卧室）	1 211.57	950—1 500
市中心公寓（3间卧室）	3 114.93	2 200—5 000
市中心以外公寓（3间卧室）	2 026.80	1 500—2 750

表5.58 公寓价格　　　　　　　　　　　　　　　单位：英镑

	每平方米均价	单价范围
在市中心购买公寓	12 939.98	9 200—17 000
在中心以外购买公寓	7 002.96	5 000—9 000

表5.59 薪资和融资

	均　值	范　围
平均月净工资（税后）	2 264.17英镑	
抵押贷款利率/20年/固定利率	3.30%	2.25%—5.00%

数据来源：numbeo；数据更新时间：2019年12月。

表5.60 国家数据

人均国内生产总值	39 953.57美元
人口增长率	0.52%

数据来源：世界银行，2019年。

【非英国居民购房政策】

对外国所有权没有任何限制。

5.3.2 专家邀稿：脱欧背景下的英国房产市场

2019年对于目光聚焦在英国房地产市场上的海外投资者来讲，最关注的怕是下面这三个词了：脱欧、大选和汇率。

虽然说2016年6月英国脱欧公投结果令众多人大跌眼镜，也给投资者的信心带来了一些负面影响，但是三年多来无休止的拖延所带来的祸害，在很多人的心里已经超越了脱欧本身的损害。"无论好坏，尽快有个结果，带有危害的定论终究比无限期的不定性要好。"我们这些英国房产界的一线工作人员听到了越来越多类似的声音。

所以"脱欧"自然而然地成为2019年英国房地产界的一个重要关注点。这一年对于英国人民来讲是个"全年无休"等待脱欧的状态，脱欧历程走得非常坎坷。

从原定的3月31日脱欧日被延期改到后来的10月（万圣节前后），脱欧一直没有明确的定论。直至12月12日（"双十二"大选），鲍里斯·约翰逊（Boris Johnson）所领导的保守党以压倒式优势获胜，成为英国现任新首相，市场才开始明朗化一些，因为他许诺将会在2020年1月31日完成脱欧。与时事相关的还有汇率的变化，2016年6月24日公投意外脱欧后，英镑对人民币一度大跌超过10%，从6月23日的9.865 0暴跌至8.747 9，此后在长达3年的时间里英镑始终乏力。2019年也是一路疲软，长期位居9以下。直至年底竞选，汇率随着保守党优势稳定的影响，市场信心逐渐上升，英镑对人民币才得以进入快速反弹通道。12月13日英镑弹至2019年最高点9.382 25。高盛最新分析也随即表示，随着英国脱欧的明朗化，英镑将成为"高盛在2020年一季度首选的G10货币"。

上述因素为背景的情况下，2019年英国住宅房产以大选为分水岭，前后出现了非常有趣的现象。

大选前，本地市场信心不足，除了出租市场较2018年有所提升以外（无论在租金水平上还是在市场活跃度上），商业地产、住宅地产本地交易量都有明显下滑趋势。这段时间市场上很大一股支撑的力量来自海外买家，中国买家在脱欧公投结果出来以后至今给英国房地产界做了不小的贡献，一方面，海外买家借用了汇率优势这个杠杆，另一方面，海外买家尤其是现金买家抓住了英国开发商的心态软肋，这期间，市场上时不时地可以看到两位数的大折扣的出现，"现金为王""资本的力量"在这个"买家市场"阶段充分得以体现。这样的行情在"双十二"鲍里斯大获全胜之后得到了逆转。综合各方公开的报道的统计，在大选结束后短短一周的时间里面，各路资本仅在伦敦就达成了20余笔大手笔交易，总投资额已过50亿英镑！

现在看来，在我们赞叹李嘉诚和每一位在这过去几年里投资英国的海外投资者明智的投资决定的同时，反过来想想，他们更值得我们赞叹的倒是他们能在情况不明朗、各种不定性层层迭合之时可以断然出手相投的勇气和魄力！

2020年鼠年将至，跨年之后除了脱欧，恐怕大家应该重点关注的一个事态就是"3%的海外买家印花税"是否会落实和何时落实了，因为这将会直接影响到所有的海外买家。如果该政策落实，那么政府有可能会在2020年预算案宣布税务更改法案生效。

2020预计有两个预算案：第一个预算在春季，可能在二月下旬或者三月上旬进行，第二个预算在秋季。那么究竟会是在哪个时间节点呢？就这个问题，世嘉置业在大选结束后第一时间访谈了英国资深税务师寻求专业观点，希望帮助持有英国房产的客户为即将到来的变化做好准备。

英国必臻会计师事务所企业税务合伙人、在英国印花税领域有近20年经验、撰写过印花税方面权威教科书、2017年年度税务作家Sean表示："对非居民征收3%附加印花税的制度非常复杂，政府需要首先发布法律草案以进行社会各界磋商，最快是在二月下旬或者三月上旬春季预算案时进行，首先发表法令草案表明想法并征求意见，然后至少要花几个月的时间对详细的法规草案进行评论。因此，我个人认为，3%附加印花税会在2020年二月份春季预算时立法生效的可能非常渺茫；甚至在2020年夏天或2021年夏天也不太现实。"

当然没有什么是完全不可能的，政府的确把3%附加印花税作为他们很大一部分的税务宣言，所以对于这个事态发展的紧密跟进，从而在投资时间上做好充分合理的规划，将会是海外买家需要重视的一个关注点。在新政落实之前的这段时间，很可能会带来一波集中购买。

通常情况下，诸如此类的所有规则都有所谓的过渡条款，意味着即使买家在立法要求的特定日期后完成交易，只要是在立法公布日前交换的合同，仍然可以避免受法律变更的影响，但是这些都不排除例外情况的发生。所以最理想情况下，出于谨慎的考虑，买家应该在春季预算案公布之前交换合同，但是也要意识到，如果交换合同之后又以某种方式修改了合同，那么买家很有可能仍然会失去这些过渡性条款的保护。

脱欧进展和汇率的波动仍然是2020年海外投资者需要关注的事项。虽然说2016年到2019年大选前海外买家汇率优势的窗口在关闭，但是脱欧谈判，脱欧过程中每每遇到难题都会给汇率带来负面的影响，希望海外买家可以继续紧密关注，善用良机。

2019年"双十二"大选给英国本地市场注入了大量信心，大选结果宣布后当天，各大开发商股票股值上涨，纷纷开始积极拿地，并为2020年房价制定商讨新的策略。脱欧后市场上可以看到的开发商给出打折扣的案例将会越来越少，本地市场交易将会日渐活跃，再加上海外买家3%印花税可能落实的风险，2020年海外投资者想要在英国入手好的项目需要采用不同的技巧和方向。

对于有长久投资规划和一次交易多套房产的买家来讲，提前设立正确的公司架构和税务规划将会变得尤其重要；对于小额投资或单套投资的买家而言，由于购买成本提升，如何选择合适的产品，如何衡量长线、中线和短线投资的利弊，如何提前考虑和安排交房后的出租管理种种琐事，将会变得至关重要。

本文作者：王静，SALLY WANG

英国世嘉置业（SJW Properties）创始人＆总经理。

王静（Sally Wang）女士在英国已经学习、工作、生活了近19年。2015年她成立了英国世嘉置业（SJW Properties），总部位于英国伦敦，在上海设有办事处，着力帮助全球华人在英国置业。英国世嘉置业多次被中英媒体播报，2019年世嘉置业被英国房产电视台评为19家最值得关注的英国房产公司之一，并已顺利入选2020年英国最值得关注的20家房产公司之一。

她写作并出版了《英国置业三部曲》（清华大学出版社）和《非凡之道》（江苏凤凰文艺出版社）（均可在中国各大线上线下书店购买）。

王静（Sally Wang）女士曾接受2015年BBC 100名优秀女性节目采访，并曾在CCTV-2，中央人民广播电台，《中国经营报》《人民日报》等对英国房地产发表专业观点。

5.3.3　德国：房价增长加速

经过四年多的强劲房价上涨，德国的住房市场仍然非常强劲。到2019年第三季度，公寓的平均价格上涨了9.46%，比上年的5.15%的增长有所改善。实际上，这是自2016年第二季度以来最大的同比增长。按季度计算，最近一个季度房价上涨了3.34%。

由于低利率、城市化和健康的家庭融资，住房需求依然强劲。最近，移民危机和强劲的经济增长增加了该国本已强劲的需求。尽管如此，建筑活动仍然疲软。根据联邦统计局（Destatis）的数据，在2019年的前八个月，住宅许可证与上年同期相比下降了2.5%，至228 500套。

柏林的公寓购买成本约为每平方米4 991欧元。在租金收益率方面，平均收益率在2.9%至3.7%之间。

根据Destatis的数据，德国经济在2018年增长乏力，实际GDP增长仅为1.4%，低于2017年的2.2%，也是五年来最弱的增长。欧洲最大的经济体2019年仍在挣扎，第一季度GDP增长仅为0.7%，第二季度为0.4%，第三季度为0.5%。从季度来看，经济在2019年第三季度几乎没有增长0.1%，在上一季度收缩0.2%之后勉强避免了技术衰退。

因此，德国对出口依赖的经济受到全球对资本货物需求下降的打击，而政治不确定性和汽车行业的结构变化增加了负担。政府最近将2019年的经济增长预期下调至0.5%，是先前预测的一半。

【德国柏林房产数据】

表5.61　主要指标

价格收入比	10.59
抵押贷款占收入的百分比	63.38%
贷款承受能力指数	1.58
市中心租金价格比	29.69

(续表)

出租价格比——中心以外	26.50
总租金收益率（市中心）	3.37%
总租金收益率（中心以外）	3.77%

表5.62　每月租金　　　　　　　　　　　　　　　　　　　　单位：欧元

	每月租金均价	租金范围
市中心公寓（1间卧室）	899.70	650—1 200
市中心以外公寓（1间卧室）	650.91	450—850
市中心公寓（3间卧室）	1 684.75	1 250—2 200
市中心以外公寓（3间卧室）	1 216.10	900—1 500

表5.63　公寓价格　　　　　　　　　　　　　　　　　　　　单位：欧元

	每平方米均价	单价范围
在市中心购买公寓	5 933.19	4 500—8 000
在中心以外购买公寓	3 828.00	3 300—4 500

表5.64　薪资和融资

	均　　值	范　　围
平均月净工资（税后）	2 305.05欧元	
抵押贷款利率/20年/固定利率	1.85%	1.4%—2.0%

数据来源：numbeo；数据更新时间：2019年12月。

表5.65　国家数据

人均国内生产总值	44 665.51美元
人口增长率	−0.16%

数据来源：世界银行，2019年。

【非德国居民购房政策】

外国公民在德国购买房地产没有任何限制。外国人可以筹措资金,但不应期望能支付超过购买价格60%的费用。

5.3.4 葡萄牙:住房市场正在加强

在需求激增和经济状况改善的推动下,葡萄牙的住房价格继续上涨。葡萄牙的房地产价格在截至2019年第三季度的一年中上涨了7.92%,高于2019年第二季度的7.38%、2019年第一季度的5.96%、2018年第四季度的5.39%和2018年第三季度的4.7%,乃十多年来的最高增长。2019年第三季度房价环比增长2.47%。

在过去的十年中,葡萄牙所有地区的房价均出现了大幅下跌。尽管2009年有所回升,但房价在2010年最后一个季度再次开始下跌。房价在连续13个季度同比下降之后,才在2014年第四季度开始回升。

需求和供应激增。根据葡萄牙国家统计局的数据,2018年葡萄牙的房屋交易总量同比增长16.6%,达到178 691套。同样,同期交易额同比增长24.4%,至240.6亿欧元(268.1亿美元)。显然,2017年推出的适用于高价值房地产的新财富税实际上对豪华住房市场的影响微不足道。

在2018年的前三个季度中,葡萄牙的许可居住证数量比上年同期猛增了19%以上,达到17 558个单位,而2018年则增长了约40%。

穆迪投资服务公司(Moody's Investors Service)预测,葡萄牙的房地产市场将保持蓬勃发展,直到2020年为止,每年的房价将上涨7%至8%。

根据葡萄牙统计局的数据,葡萄牙经济在2019年第三季度同比增长1.9%,与上一季度持平。因此,国际货币基金组织(IMF)最近将其对葡萄牙经济的2019年增长预测从先前的1.7%上调至1.9%。

【葡萄牙里斯本房产数据】

表5.66 主要指标

指标	数值
价格收入比	17.97
抵押贷款占收入的百分比	109.52%
贷款承受能力指数	0.91
市中心租金价格比	21.34
出租价格比——中心以外	17.42
总租金收益率(市中心)	4.69%
总租金收益率(中心以外)	5.74%

表5.67　每月租金　　　　　　　　　　　　　　　　　　　　　　　单位：欧元

	每月租金均价	租金范围
市中心公寓（1间卧室）	884.67	600—1 100
市中心以外公寓（1间卧室）	615.13	400—800
市中心公寓（3间卧室）	1 712.08	1 300—2 200
市中心以外公寓（3间卧室）	1 137.30	800—1 500

表5.68　公寓价格　　　　　　　　　　　　　　　　　　　　　　　单位：欧元

	每平方米均价	单价范围
在市中心购买公寓	4 257.81	3 000—6 000
在中心以外购买公寓	2 366.35	1 500—3 500

表5.69　薪资和融资

	均　　值	范　　围
平均月净工资（税后）	921.62欧元	
抵押贷款利率/20年/固定利率	2.04%	1.25%—3.0%

数据来源：numbeo；数据更新时间：2019年12月。

表5.70　国家数据

人均国内生产总值	21 291.43美元
人口增长率	0.04%

数据来源：世界银行，2019年。

【非葡萄牙居民购房政策】

对外国财产所有权没有限制。

5.3.5　西班牙：住房市场保持健康

西班牙房屋价格在2019年第二季度同比上涨2.08%，此前2019年第一季度同比增长2.53%；

2018年第四季度为5.25%，第三季度为2.39%，第二季度为4.01%，第一季度为2.37%。2019年第二季度房价环比小幅下降0.15%。

在经历了八年的房价下跌之后，西班牙的房地产市场终于在2016年第一季度恢复增长。根据西班牙不动产估价局（TINSA）的数据，西班牙的房价从2007年第四季度到2015年第三季度共下跌了41.9%（经通胀调整后为46.8%）。连续31个季度同比下降。

需求和供应仍然强劲。根据西班牙国家统计研究所（INE）的数据，西班牙的房屋销售在2018年同比增长10.3%，2017年同比增长15.4%，2016年同比增长14%，2015年同比增长11.5%。交易量持续增长的主要原因是，外国人在沿海地区以及巴塞罗那和太阳海岸等城市购买房屋，该国房产深受海外购买者的欢迎。大多数外国购房者是英国人、法国人、德国人、比利时人、意大利人和瑞典人。

由于需求上升，建筑活动再次升温。2018年期间，住宅建筑许可证数量分别增长10.6%，至27 584个单位。

【西班牙马德里房产数据】

表5.71 主要指标

价格收入比	12.54
抵押贷款占收入的百分比	77.4%
贷款承受能力指数	1.29
市中心租金价格比	25.99
出租价格比——中心以外	20.43
总租金收益率（市中心）	3.85%
总租金收益率（中心以外）	4.89%

表5.72 每月租金　　　　　　　　　　　　　　　　单位：欧元

	每月租金均价	租金范围
市中心公寓（1间卧室）	915.38	700—1 200
市中心以外公寓（1间卧室）	691.17	500—890
市中心公寓（3间卧室）	1 617.46	1 200—2 014.05
市中心以外公寓（3间卧室）	1 093.32	850—1 500

表5.73 公寓价格　　　　　　　　　　　　　　　　　　　　　　　　　单位：欧元

	每平方米均价	单价范围
在市中心购买公寓	5 147.83	3 500—7 000
在中心以外购买公寓	2 913.08	2 000—4 000

表5.74 薪资和融资

	均　值	范　围
平均月净工资（税后）	1 606.53欧元	
抵押贷款利率/20年/固定利率	2.18%	1.90%—2.90%

数据来源：numbeo；数据更新时间：2019年12月。

表5.75 国家数据

人均国内生产总值	21 291.43美元
人口增长率	0.04%

数据来源：世界银行，2019年。

【非西班牙居民购房政策】

外国人有权无限制地购买和转售各种财产——住宅、商业或土地。

5.3.6 瑞典：房价再次上涨

在连续五个季度年度价格下跌之后，瑞典全国房价指数在截至2019年第三季度的一年中上涨了2.09%。在最近一个季度，房屋价格比上一季度增长了1.91%。

需求稳定，供应下降。根据瑞典统计局的数据，在2019年的前三个季度中，一栋至两栋住宅的房屋销量同比增长0.2%，至39 764套，比上年同期下降了1.2%。在2019年的前三个季度中，新建的一到两栋房屋的住宅开工量同比下降20%，至约6 931套；同样，住宅完工量也下降了21.5%，至7 016套。

国家经济研究所（NIER）将瑞典2019年的增长预测从先前的1.5%下调至仅1.2%，理由是贸易战升级，英国退欧协议和中东冲突升级导致不确定性增加。NIER预计2020年增长会进一步放缓。

【瑞典斯德哥尔摩房产数据】

表5.76 主要指标

价格收入比	14.29
抵押贷款占收入的百分比	90.78%
贷款承受能力指数	1.10

(续表)

市中心租金价格比	36.02
出租价格比——中心以外	32.53
总租金收益率（市中心）	2.78%
总租金收益率（中心以外）	3.07%

表5.77　每月租金　　　　　　　　　　　　　　　单位：瑞典克朗

	每月租金均价	租金范围
市中心公寓（1间卧室）	12 311.88	7 000—15 628.99
市中心以外公寓（1间卧室）	8 438.63	5 000—12 000
市中心公寓（3间卧室）	20 333.33	12 000—26 000
市中心以外公寓（3间卧室）	12 584.29	8 400—18 000

表5.78　公寓价格　　　　　　　　　　　　　　　单位：瑞典克朗

	每平方米均价	单价范围
在市中心购买公寓	93 158.55	80 000—102 000
在中心以外购买公寓	55 269.18	40 000—75 000

表5.79　薪资和融资

	均　　值	范　　围
平均月净工资（税后）	25 967.07瑞典克朗	
抵押贷款利率/20年/固定利率	2.49%	1.70%—3.30%

数据来源：numbeo；数据更新时间：2019年12月。

表5.80　国家数据

人均国内生产总值	53 253.48美元
人口增长率	0.81%

数据来源：世界银行，2019年。

【非瑞典居民购房政策】

外国人在瑞典购买房地产没有法律限制。

5.3.7 俄罗斯：住房市场改善

俄罗斯的房价在截至2019年第三季度的一年中上涨了3.63%，与上年同期0.18%的涨幅相比有大幅改善，是自2012年第四季度以来的最高增幅。最近一个季度，全国房价上涨了1.69%。莫斯科的价格在2019年第三季度同比增长5.49%，而在圣彼得堡则猛增9.47%。

在过去的七年中，俄罗斯房价下跌了47%（经通货膨胀调整后）。

不过，俄罗斯的经济现在正在显著改善。通货膨胀现在趋于稳定。根据联邦国家统计局（Federal State Statistics Service）的数据，2019年10月，总体通货膨胀率放缓至3.8%，为当年最低水平，在央行设定的4%目标之内。在通胀压力放缓的情况下，俄罗斯中央银行（CBR）于2019年10月将其主要利率降低了50个基点，至6.5%，这是2019年第四次降息。关键利率在2014年12月达到峰值17%。

2019年10月，平均每月汇率为64.329卢布＝1美元——从年初以来升值约5%。卢布在短短三年内就贬值了近61%，从2013年1月的30.231卢布＝1美元的汇率，跌至2016年1月的77.175卢布＝1美元。然后在2018年，卢布贬值了近16%，再次抵消了2016年和2017年31.5%的增长。

【俄罗斯莫斯科房产数据】

表5.81 主要指标

价格收入比	19.75
抵押贷款占收入的百分比	232.67%
贷款承受能力指数	0.43
市中心租金价格比	24.62
出租价格比——中心以外	21.74
总租金收益率（市中心）	4.06%
总租金收益率（中心以外）	4.60%

表5.82 每月租金　　　　　　　　　　　　　　　　　　　　单位：卢布

	每月租金均价	租金范围
市中心公寓（1间卧室）	60 941.18	50 000—80 000
市中心以外公寓（1间卧室）	35 315.50	30 000—45 000
市中心公寓（3间卧室）	125 257.17	90 000—200 000
市中心以外公寓（3间卧室）	67 300.00	50 000—90 000

表5.83 公寓价格　　　　　　　　　　　　　　　　　　　　　　　单位：卢布

	每平方米均价	单价范围
在市中心购买公寓	348 250.96	250 000—500 000
在中心以外购买公寓	171 965.07	120 000—220 000

表5.84 薪资和融资

	均　　值	范　　围
平均月净工资（税后）	65 839.04卢布	
抵押贷款利率/20年/固定利率	10.25%	9.0%—11.50%

数据来源：numbeo；数据更新时间：2019年12月。

表5.85 国家数据

人均国内生产总值	10 743.10美元
人口增长率	−0.08%

数据来源：世界银行，2019年。

【非俄罗斯居民购房政策】

2001年的立法使房地产向外国投资开放。2001年的《土地法》允许当地人和外国人私有土地和财产。在《俄罗斯土地法典》颁布之前，不允许私有土地，只能租用49年的土地。

在《土地法》颁布之前，土地所有权与使用权（财产）不同。所有权和使用权之间的这种区别阻碍了俄罗斯房地产市场的平稳发展。《土地法》整合了土地所有权和使用权。但是，在某些情况下，立法没有得到认真执行，外国人仍然无法渗透莫斯科的土地市场。

5.3.8　希腊：房价再次上涨

希腊在经历了七年的房价下跌之后，由于经济条件的改善，情况开始好转。根据希腊银行（Bank of Greece）的数据，在希腊市区，截至2018年第三季度，房价上涨了2.51%，是自2008年第一季度以来的年度最高涨幅。扣除通胀因素后，房价上涨了1.53%。2018年第三季度，市区房价环比增长1.2%（实际价格为2.01%）。

在主要城市中也看到了这种改善：

雅典以2018年第三季度的年度房价上涨3.71%（实际价值为2.71%）引领了该国的住房市场。实际上，这是自2007年第四季度以来首都的最佳表现。在最近一个季度中，房价上涨了1.65%（实际价值为2.48%）。

在该国第二大城市塞萨洛尼基,2018年第三季度房价同比增长1.9%(按实际价值计算为0.9%),而上年同期则为1.3%,这是自2008年第一季度以来的最高增幅。价格在2018年第三季度小幅上涨了0.5%(实际价值为1.3%)。

在其他城市(不包括雅典和塞萨洛尼基),到2018年第三季度,房价上涨了1.2%(实际价值为0.2%),高于上年同期的0.5%的同比下降。按季度计算,2018年第三季度价格上涨了0.6%(实际价值为1.4%)。

从2008年到2017年,希腊住宅房地产价格下降了42.7%(实际价值为-46.3%)。

在2018年的前八个月中,雅典土地注册处记录的住宅物业转让数量比上年同期增长了59.6%。

根据希腊统计局的数据,在2018年的前9个月中,建筑许可的总数比上年同期增长了9%,达到10 817个单位。但它仍然远远低于2004年至2007年每年颁发的7万至8万份许可。

为了振兴房地产市场,希腊政府向非欧盟投资者提供了购买或租赁价值25万欧元以上房产的居所。居住计划类似于匈牙利、西班牙和葡萄牙采取的措施。该计划有效期为五年,可以更新。

但是,希腊的高物业税继续抑制需求。实际上,自全球金融危机以来,财产税增长了七倍。在2018年,希腊的630万房地产所有者被要求支付总计31.5亿欧元的财产税(ENFIA),而2009年为5亿欧元。租金税也有所增加。对于低于12 000欧元的年租金收入,税率为15%。对于每年12 000欧元至35 000欧元的租金收入,税率飙升至35%。

【希腊雅典房产数据】

表5.86 主要指标

价格收入比	11.08
抵押贷款占收入的百分比	86.02%
贷款承受能力指数	1.16
市中心租金价格比	22.13
出租价格比——中心以外	23.48
总租金收益率(市中心)	4.52%
总租金收益率(中心以外)	4.26%

表5.87 每月租金　　　　　　　　　　　　　　　　　　单位:欧元

	每月租金均价	租金范围
市中心公寓(1间卧室)	374.69	300—500
市中心以外公寓(1间卧室)	338.54	250—400
市中心公寓(3间卧室)	670.62	500—900
市中心以外公寓(3间卧室)	606.00	450—800

表5.88 公寓价格　　　　　　　　　　　　　　　　　　　　　　　　　　　　单位：欧元

	每平方米均价	单价范围
在市中心购买公寓	1 804.84	1 200—3 000
在中心以外购买公寓	1 730.06	1 000—2 500

5.89 薪资和融资

	均　　值	范　　围
平均月净工资（税后）	797.59欧元	
抵押贷款利率/20年/固定利率	4.76%	3.5%—6.0%

数据来源：numbeo；数据更新时间：2019年12月。

表5.90 国家数据

人均国内生产总值	18 885.48美元
人口增长率	−0.06%

数据来源：世界银行，2019年。

【非希腊居民购房政策】

欧盟国民可以在希腊自由购买财产，而非欧盟国民则有一些限制。潜在买家必须开立希腊银行账户，并转移购买所需的所有资金（物业价格、公证费、注册费等），以便符合希腊税法或以其他方式通过希腊进口海关总署。在军事基地、国界附近（主要是出于安全原因，尤其是在土耳其附近的边界）和某些岛屿中的财产获得，需要获得地方委员会的特别许可。此类许可不授予非欧盟国民。

5.3.9　土耳其：真实房价暴跌

根据土耳其共和国中央银行（CBRT）的数据，截至2018年11月的一年中，土耳其全国房价指数上涨了10.5%。但是，扣除通货膨胀因素，它们同比下降了9.2%。比上年同期通货膨胀调整后的价格下降1.5%的幅度下降更大。

土耳其住宅的总销售量也下降了，在2018年下降了2.41%。此外，土耳其里拉兑美元的价格已经大幅下跌，这有助于外国购买房地产者的大量增加。

在土耳其最大的城市伊斯坦布尔，截至2018年11月的一年中，名义房屋价格上涨了6.3%。但扣除通货膨胀因素后，房屋价格实际上同比下降了12.6%。在该国首都安卡拉，2018年11月房价同比上涨8.9%。但是，经通胀调整后，房价下跌了10.5%。

【土耳其伊斯坦布尔房产数据】

表5.91　主要指标

价格收入比	11.34
抵押贷款占收入的百分比	235.94%
贷款承受能力指数	0.42
市中心租金价格比	20.66
出租价格比——中心以外	17.53
总租金收益率（市中心）	4.84%
总租金收益率（中心以外）	5.70%

表5.92　每月租金　　　　　　　　　　　　　　　　单位：里拉

	每月租金均价	租金范围
市中心公寓（1间卧室）	1 930.77	1 500—2 500
市中心以外公寓（1间卧室）	1 163.07	800—1 500
市中心公寓（3间卧室）	3 593.78	2 500—5 000
市中心以外公寓（3间卧室）	2 035.05	1 500—2 750

表5.93　公寓价格　　　　　　　　　　　　　　　　单位：里拉

	每平方米均价	单价范围
在市中心购买公寓	8 835.90	5 500—15 000
在中心以外购买公寓	4 392.75	2 625—6 000

表5.94　薪资和融资

	均　　值	范　　围
平均月净工资（税后）	2 917.17里拉	
抵押贷款利率/20年/固定利率	20.45%	15.0%—25.0%

数据来源：numbeo；数据更新时间：2019年12月。

表5.95 国家数据

人均国内生产总值	10 546.15美元
人口增长率	0.52%

数据来源：世界银行，2019年。

【非土耳其居民购房政策】

土耳其的外国所有权受互惠原则管辖。允许土耳其公民或法人在其国家拥有财产的国家公民，可以在土耳其获得财产。大多数欧盟国家（比利时、塞浦路斯、捷克共和国和斯洛伐克除外）、美国、加拿大以及亚洲、拉丁美洲和非洲的其他国家的公民都可以自由购买土耳其的房地产。

外国公民在注册人口少于2 000人的市政区域内购买房产受到限制（《乡村法》第87条），也不允许外国人在军区范围内购买房产（《军事禁止和安全区法》）。2006年1月7日，颁布了一项新法律，限制了外国人可以购买的土地数量。外国人最多可以购买30公顷（74英亩）的房地产。购买任何一块超过30公顷的土地都需要获得土耳其当局的许可。

5.3.10 马耳他：房价持续强劲上涨

马耳他中央银行(CBM)的数据显示，截至2019年第一季度，马耳他的房价仍上涨了10.83%（经通胀调整后为9.51%）。最近一个季度，房地产价格上涨了4.72%（经通胀调整后为6.56%）。

截至2019年第一季度，公寓平均价格上涨了11.02%。扣除通胀因素后，价格上涨了9.7%。

马耳他在过去五年中的房价强劲上涨受到多种因素的支持。根据CBM的2018年年度报告，2014年和2015年平均增长率为9.6%，其次2016年至2018年为6.3%。低利率环境、可支配收入的增长以及该国外籍工人的数量不断增加，都是支撑房价上涨的因素。

同时，政府措施还提振了房价，其中包括对首次购房者免除新房产首15万欧元的3.5%印花税。2018年，又推出了一项计划，使第二次购房者如果打算更换当前的住宅房屋，则有资格获得高达3 000欧元的印花税退款。如果第二次购房者拥有其他财产，或正在升级为豪华别墅，则没有资格。残疾房主可以申请最高5 000欧元的印花税退款。

毫无疑问，近年来房价的上涨还归功于政府2013年11月预算中引入的针对高净值个人的个人投资者计划(IIP)。

从2000年到2007年，马耳他房地产市场一直保持强劲增长，整体房价指数上涨了78.9%（经通胀调整后为53.4%）；排屋价格涨幅最大，达105.3%（经通胀调整后为76%）；公寓价格上涨83.3%（经通胀调整后为57.1%）；小别墅的价格上涨了81.4%（经通胀调整后为55.5%）；联排别墅和别墅上涨71.9%（经通胀调整后为47.4%）。

与其他欧洲国家一样，马耳他也受到了2008年全球金融危机的打击。在2011年短暂复苏之后，2012年房价再次下跌了2.2%（经通胀调整后为−5.2%）。

由于政府推出了与房地产相关的新措施，房价于2013年强劲反弹。从2014年到2018年，价格持续强劲上涨。

【马耳他瓦莱塔房产数据】

表5.96 主要指标

价格收入比	13.81
抵押贷款占收入的百分比	104.43%
贷款承受能力指数	0.96
市中心租金价格比	18.86
出租价格比——中心以外	12.01
总租金收益率（市中心）	5.3%
总租金收益率（中心以外）	8.32%

表5.97 每月租金　　　　　　　　　　　　　　　　单位：欧元

	每月租金均价	租金范围
市中心公寓（1间卧室）	954.55	700—1 200
市中心以外公寓（1间卧室）	759.65	500—1 000
市中心公寓（3间卧室）	1 836.36	1 200—3 000
市中心以外公寓（3间卧室）	1 304.55	900—2 000

表5.98 公寓价格　　　　　　　　　　　　　　　　单位：欧元

	每平方米均价	单价范围
在市中心购买公寓	4 050.00	2 500—5 000
在中心以外购买公寓	1 950.00	1 500—7 000

表5.99 薪资和融资

	均　　值	范　　围
平均月净工资（税后）	1 085.83欧元	
抵押贷款利率/20年/固定利率	4.45%	3.0%—8.0%

数据来源：numbeo；数据更新时间：2019年12月。

表5.100　国家数据

人均国内生产总值	26 748.21美元
人口增长率	0.26%

数据来源：世界银行，2019年。

【非马耳他居民购房政策】

欧盟公民可以在马耳他或戈佐岛购买一处房产，在"特别指定地区"可以购买更多房产，例如蒂涅角、波托马索、卡内塔拉、马努埃尔岛和昌布雷。

所购买的财产只能作为所有者或其直系亲属的住所使用。带有游泳池的别墅除外。另外，只能在该国居住至少连续五年后才能购买第二套房产。

非欧盟公民的其他外国公民必须从财政部获得不动产购置许可证（AIP），处理通常需要三个月的时间。要获得AIP许可，您的预期财产的购买价格必须至少为69 900欧元（公寓）或116 500欧元。

准买家还必须能够证明所使用的资金已从国外汇出（即银行收据）。AIP许可证仅允许您购买和拥有一处住宅物业，供您和您家庭的个人使用。只有在以下特定指定区域中才能购买其他物业：Portomaso，Tigne Project，Cottonera Waterfront和Gozo的Charmai。

5.4 北美地区

5.4.1 美国:房价继续上涨 增速有所放缓

在连续六年强劲的房价增长之后,美国住房市场正在降温。S & P / Case-Shiller季节性调整后的全国房价指数在截至2019年第二季度的一年中仅上涨了1.46%(经通胀调整),这是自2012年第三季度以来的最低增幅。联邦住房金融局(FHFA)公布的经季节性调整的仅购买美国房屋价格指数在2019年第二季度同比增长3.12%(经通胀调整),是近五年来的最低增幅。在最近一个季度,FHFA指数环比小幅下降0.15%。

需求和建筑活动继续增加。根据美国人口普查局的数据,2019年7月,新单户住宅的销售同比增长4.3%,达到季节性调整后的63.5万套的年率。另一方面,同期的成屋销售同比小幅增长0.6%,达到了季节性调整后的年率542万套。2019年7月,新房屋开工量同比略增0.6%,至经季节性调整的年率111.1万套,而竣工量增长6.3%,至1 250 000套。同样,2019年7月,获准用于新住房的建筑许可同比增长1.5%,达到1 336 000套的年化率。

根据美国房屋建筑商协会(NAHB)/ Wells Fargo房屋市场指数(HMI)的数据,在抵押贷款利率下降的情况下,2019年8月美国房屋建筑商的情绪仍然高居66点,较上个月高出一个百分点。读数50是积极情绪和消极情绪之间的中点。

【美国纽约房产数据】

表5.101　主要指标

价格收入比	11.04
抵押贷款占收入的百分比	81.08%
贷款承受能力指数	1.22
市中心租金价格比	20.29
出租价格比——中心以外	16.99
总租金收益率（市中心）	4.93%
总租金收益率（中心以外）	5.88%

表5.102　每月租金　　　　　　　　　　　　　　　　单位：美元

	每月租金均价	租金范围
市中心公寓（1间卧室）	3 082.33	2 300—4 000
市中心以外公寓（1间卧室）	2 009.66	1 500—2 500
市中心公寓（3间卧室）	6 249.60	4 000—9 000
市中心以外公寓（3间卧室）	3 700.00	2 500—5 000

表5.103　公寓价格　　　　　　　　　　　　　　　　单位：美元

	每平方米均价	单价范围
在市中心购买公寓	14 422.10	10 763.91—20 000.00
在中心以外购买公寓	7 527.25	3 767.37—11 840.30

表5.104　薪资和融资

	均　　值	范　　围
平均月净工资（税后）	4 968.63美元	
抵押贷款利率/20年/固定利率	4.21%	3.50%—4.50%

数据来源：numbeo；数据更新时间：2019年12月。

表5.105　国家数据

人均国内生产总值	59 927.93美元
人口增长率	0.81%

数据来源：世界银行，2019年。

【非美国居民购房政策】

对外资在美国拥有房地产的限制很少，对于从购买到出租的投资目的来说微不足道。在联邦一级，对拥有或投资不动产的非居民外国人（NRA）仅有几项限制（1978年《农业外国投资披露法》（FIDA）；1976年《国际投资调查法》（IISA）；《1980年房地产投资税法》（FIRPTA））。出于实际目的，这些限制并不重要。在俄克拉荷马州，不允许外国人购买土地，但他们可以购买公寓。

5.4.2　加拿大：房价下跌

截至2019年第二季度，加拿大11个主要城市的房价下跌了1.48%。这是连续第二个季度同比下降，是市场自2009年第二季度以来最差的表现。在2019年第二季度，房屋价格环比小幅上涨0.53%。

房屋销售再次上升；建筑活动仍然疲软。2019年7月的实际销售活动比上年同期增长12.6%。根据加拿大房地产协会（CREA）的数据，主要是由于不列颠哥伦比亚省、卡尔加里、埃德蒙顿、大多伦多地区以及汉密尔顿-伯灵顿、渥太华和蒙特利尔的低陆平原地区。与之相比，2018年的销售额下降了11.2%。

根据加拿大抵押和住房公司（CMHC）的数据，2019年前七个月的住宅开工量同比下降1.9%，至109 703套，竣工数量同比下降3.5%，至102 694套。

加拿大经济在2018年增长了1.8%，较2017年的3%增速有所放缓，这主要是由于其石油和天然气行业疲软。加拿大银行（BoC）预计2019年经济增长将进一步放缓至1.3%。自2017年7月以来五次上调利率后，加拿大银行（BoC）于2019年7月将其关键利率保持在1.75%不变。

【加拿大温哥华房产数据】

表5.106　主要指标

价格收入比	14.58
抵押贷款占收入的百分比	104.01%
贷款承受能力指数	0.96
市中心租金价格比	27.62
出租价格比——中心以外	27.22
总租金收益率（市中心）	3.62%
总租金收益率（中心以外）	3.67%

表5.107　每月租金　　　　　　　　　　　　　　　　　　　　　　　　　　单位：加元

	每月租金均价	租金范围
市中心公寓（1间卧室）	2 052.53	1 700—2 400
市中心以外公寓（1间卧室）	1 654.04	1 250—1 900
市中心公寓（3间卧室）	3 752.78	3 000—5 000
市中心以外公寓（3间卧室）	2 696.45	2 000—3 500

表5.108　公寓价格　　　　　　　　　　　　　　　　　　　　　　　　　　单位：加元

	每平方米均价	单价范围
在市中心购买公寓	12 458.81	10 763.91—16 145.87
在中心以外购买公寓	9 406.68	6 996.54—13 000

表5.109　薪资和融资

	均　　值	范　　围
平均月净工资（税后）	3 748.32加元	
抵押贷款利率/20年/固定利率	3.78%	3.05%—4.50%

数据来源：numbeo；数据更新时间：2019年12月。

表5.110　国家数据

人均国内生产总值	44 870.78美元
人口增长率	0.73%

数据来源：世界银行，2019年。

【非加拿大居民购房政策】

外国人在加拿大购买房地产实际上没有任何限制。2017年4月20日，加拿大安大略省财政厅公布了一条重磅消息，对外国购房者加征15%海外买家税。BC省的海外买家投机税现在为20%。

5.4.3　专家邀稿：温哥华房产市场投资价值分析

（1）2019年温哥华房产市场概况

● **价格变动**

2019年大温哥华地区各市的整体房价小幅下滑，市场继续保持向均衡进行调整。按照2019年

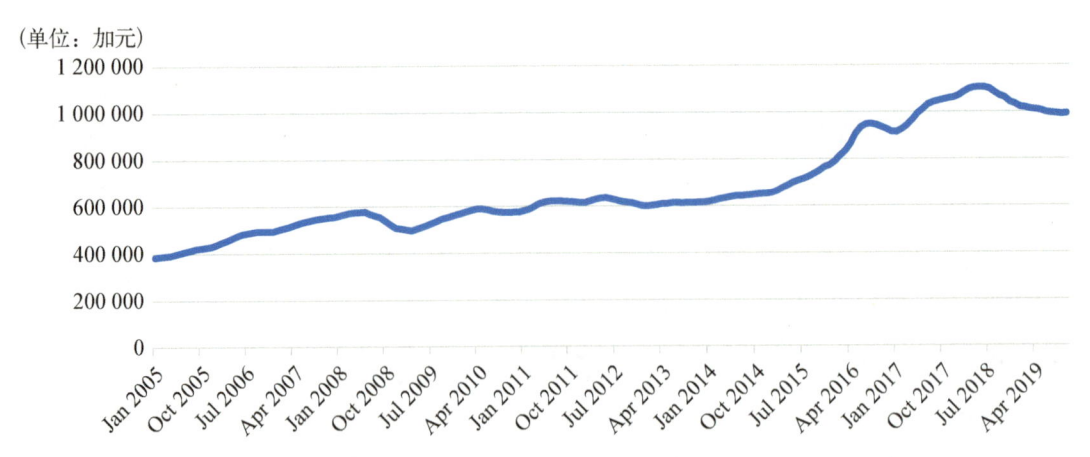

图5.1 大温哥华地区基准房价（2005年至2019年）

底的官方数据显示，大温地区整体的房价下滑了4.6%左右。基准房价自2017年5月以来首次下降至100万加元以下。年末达到99.3万加元，附带私有土地的独栋别墅价格的跌幅要超过共管物业型的联排别墅和公寓。目前在大温哥华地区，独立屋的基准价格，或者说购买一栋典型的（中等水平的）、附带自己私人土地的独立屋，要花费141.54万加元，同比下降5.8%；物业共管性质的联排别墅基准价格77.28万加元，同比下降4.4%；同为物业共管性质的公寓基准价格65.15万加元，同比下降3.8%。而在市区之间的对比中，传统高价区如温哥华西区的基准房价下滑5.3%，其中独立屋下降高达9.3%，而不允许兴建联排别墅、公寓数量也比较少的西温哥华市的基准房价降幅更是达到7.6%。上述两个区都是温哥华千万级别豪宅的主要集中地带。可以看出，尽管房价下滑的趋势整体很明显，但绝大部分下滑压力来源于价格昂贵的独立屋，相对来说，联排别墅和公寓更加适应刚需，首次购房者更青睐的物业下降的幅度并不那么明显。

- **交易情况**

市场的交易量也为温哥华房地产市场趋向调整做出了佐证。2019年夏天过后，在价格相对稳定的9月、10月和11月，房屋的整体销售量相比2018年同比大幅增长了50%上下，买卖双方终于在价格上达成了更多一致。卖方不再坚持2017年或者2018年的偏高要价，而买家也更多接受了现有价格平稳的现实，开始出手进入市场。

房产交易最活跃的温哥华、列治文、本那比和素里等几个主要市区基本都出现了交易量回升的迹象。市场基本上从卖家市场过渡到均衡位置。但随着交易量的回升，很多没有进入市场的观望者也开始行动，这种情况增加了市场中的新房源。甚至一些对市场很不敏感的卖家也感受到风向的变化，开始调整销售策略。

随着均衡市场的逐渐成型，刚需自住的买家目前也开始更多地出现在市场当中。其中尤其是以小换大类型的买家最为活跃，很多人趁机对自住房进行升级，将公寓换成面积更大的联排别墅或者独立屋，或者将小面积的房屋换成大屋，还有一些人尝试从较偏僻的地区搬到交通更方便、社区资源更多、学区更好的高价区。他们发现来自投资性买家的竞争开始松动，尽管自己现有的房产可能卖不到市场高点的价位，但自己换房的目标区域可能降价的幅度更大，这给了他们运作的空间。

5 全球房产市场篇

- **政策变动**

首先从政府方面,投机空置税是2019年整个不列颠哥伦比亚省(BC)房地产市场最大的变数。虽然这项税法早在一两年前就已经传出很多信息,但绝大部分居民都是在2月税法正式实施之后才切实感受到新税的影响。税法的主要征收目标是BC省内房产的海外投资者和不在BC省居住、缴纳税款的房产投资者。尽管税法包括很多豁免条例,但仍然有相当数量的房主需要缴纳房产总值0.5%~2%的惩罚性税务。此外,温哥华市独立的房屋空置税也在2019年开始正式施行,虽然政策表面上与省政府的投机空置税类似,都旨在将很多空置的房屋投入租赁市场。但此类政策对于某些投资者来说,就意味着持有房产的运营成本和需要的精力增加,这变相推动了更多卖家出售房产。2016年开始实施的海外买家房产交易附加税目前也已经从最初的15%增加到20%。这项政策仍然限制着海外买家进入市场。

从政策动机的角度讲,尽管目前温哥华的房价已经有明显的下滑,而且整体市场的均衡也已经被大众接受,但省、市甚至加拿大联邦政府整体对于限制房价,或者说惩罚房产投机者的政策倾向并没有减弱。加拿大央行目前对于利率的预期相对稳定,但仍有短期内降息的可能。加元自2014年以来,就再也没有回到过去的高汇率水平。2015年开始刺激加拿大房价飞涨的因素仍在,所以短期内,没有哪个决策者会放宽对房市的限制。

当然除了限制房产投机、房价不受控制增长的政策外,我们还可以明显地看出,新政策中也包括一些"劫富济贫"的现象。具体表现如温哥华最近将房价超过300万加元的部分所征收的房产转让税从原来的3%提高到5%。这就意味着在交易一栋400万加元的房产时,超过300万加元的那100万加元,买家需要比原来多缴纳2%,即2万加元。这当然不是一笔小钱。但此类政策的出现并不奇怪。从政治家的角度考虑,有房的富裕阶级提供的选票远远比不上购房存在困难的年轻人和低收入群体。温哥华的房价目前虽然下滑,但相较2015年初房价大涨之前仍然有大约30%的上涨。但另一方面,温哥华当地的工资水平却并没有那么大的上涨。所以从这个角度,政府也有理由在未来的一段时间之内,对房市继续保持谨慎的态度。

并不是所有的政策都对市场不利,我们前面提到加拿大央行近期可能降息。实际上我们从各大商业银行了解到,加拿大住房贷款的商业利率仍然处在发达国家中最低的水平,约为2.5%到3%之间。住房贷款的实际审批也相对宽松。相比2015年之前,住房贷款的审批的确增加了一些难度,但那些有足够实力的申请者,仍然能获得来自银行的资金支持。这对于房地产市场的交易量有一定的支撑作用。需要贷款的购房者能够获得更大的预算空间,而卖房者也较少因为贷款问题失去有强烈意向的买主。

- **国外买家**

温哥华的海外买家仍然受到很多额外税务的影响。我们前面说过,目前海外买家在购买房产时,需要缴纳房价20%的额外惩罚性税收,仅这一笔费用就足以吓退很多没有加拿大身份的购买者。但与世界上其他城市相比,温哥华的房市目前仍然存在一定的优势。加元目前的疲软状态,使加拿大的资产相对便宜。而温哥华的整体售租比仍然超过3%,部分交通便利的地区达到或接近4%,购买当地房屋出租仍然基本上足以支付房贷。同时出租又可以避免缴纳投机空置税和空屋税。权衡利弊之后,仍然有一些海外投资者继续在温哥华地区活跃。

（2）2020年温哥华房产市场影响因素及展望

- BC省新一届政府选举

因素影响力：直接、较大。

因素影响倾向：正面。

2020年温哥华将面临几个来自本地和海外的冲击。首先在5月，BC省将会举行新一届政府选举。现任省政府执政党NDP在上次大选中并没有获得最多的票数，是依靠与绿党的合作才险险拿到执政权。过去四年中，NDP的政策施行褒贬不一，能否在下届继续执政尚不明确。所以下半年房市可能还会面临一定程度的政策不确定性。

从政策上看，NDP目前对房市的态度比自由党更为谨慎、严格。如果自由党重掌大权，房市可能会有一些政策方面的宽松。即使NDP继续执政，现有的局面也不太可能继续恶化。

- 美国2020年大选

因素影响力：间接，适中，偏向影响买家。

因素影响倾向：不定。

美国2020年的大选对于包括温哥华房市在内的整个加拿大经济市场都存在很大影响。加拿大进出口贸易高度依赖美国，50%以上的贸易活动是与美国进行的。美国是温哥华海外投资者的最大源头之一，同时，很多温哥华企业与美国有合作关系，很多美国企业在温哥华设有分支机构。所以美国政治舞台在2020年末的剧情，也可能成为温哥华房市未来走向的一个间接因素。

特朗普四年前的上台对于美国经济的影响充满了不确定因素，那么他如果离任，不确定因素的出现概率应该至少与上台时相似。

- 横山油管扩建计划

因素影响力：直接，小，局部。

因素影响倾向：负面。

经历重重波折的横山油管扩建计划，终于在温哥华开始施工。从本地角度，这个项目虽然会一定程度影响极少部分的房地产购买热情，但目前可观测到的影响力并不足以单独研究。影响范围也仅限于距离油管最近数个街区而已。

- 阿省希望独立的声音

因素影响力：未知，间接。

因素影响倾向：未知。

目前存在没有太多根据，但网络上在2019年加拿大联邦大选之后曾经出现过一些骚动。加拿大传统的产油省阿尔伯塔，因为联邦的大选结果不如意，表现出希望独立的声音。如果事态闹大，这将是继魁北克法语省份之后第二个强烈表示过独立倾向的省份。阿尔伯塔省人口相对稀少，但却是加拿大原油最主要的产地。人口稀少导致阿省在联邦大选中影响力微小，但该省对于加拿大整个经济的影响力却很大。这使得当地人民对现有的政治格局不满。我们对于这种情况暂时还不会太过认真，但作为一个未来的潜在不确定因素来源，需要给予一定程度的警惕。

整体来说，我们仍然倾向于认为温哥华2020年的房价将会在平稳中继续调整。基于2019年下半年出现的交易量增加，2020年温哥华的房价走势相对乐观，预计可能有0~5%的涨幅。

(3)温哥华房产选择指南

● **投资**

对于投资者来说,温哥华目前的市场上可选的房源质量整体处于一个历史均衡水平上。楼花、公寓等相对低价的房产所获得的出租收益基本上可以满足贷款开销。不过按照现有的价格,短期内出现价值上巨大涨幅的可能性不大。建议将其看作中长期持有的投资产品。作为预售资产的楼花可能需要至少一到两年的时间交房之后才能出租,这增加了资金流通的难度,需要考虑投资者的资金链情况。而现房相对来说更容易操作,从实际情况来说,目前公寓现房也是市场上最主流的产品。

土地是另外一项重要的投资标的。我们这里所说的土地投资,主要是一些老旧的独立屋地产。房屋本身的价值已经很少,但土地本身却存在更大的投资价值。目前的市场下,推荐的主要是一些交通便利、生活质量较高社区的旧房土地。这类土地投资对于资金链的要求较高。一方面,此类投资通常需要投资者购买之后进行拆屋、重建的工作,温哥华此类活动的周期一般在一两年之间。另一方面,除了购买土地的价格之外,重建的费用也需要提前准备好,且只有购买土地的款项可以申请住房贷款。按照温哥华现在市场的价格水平,至少需要准备100万加元以上的现金才可能实施。如果要选择温哥华市等豪宅区,那么投资的准备金至少要翻番。

商业地产也是温哥华投资者可供选择的投资标的之一。目前状况下,商业地产的可选范围很大,从十几万的小摊位到几千万的厂房、农地都有可选房源。这是一个具体问题具体分析的类别,建议投资者对不同产品进行了解的同时,寻求有商业地产投资丰富经验的专业人士协助。

● **自住**

温哥华目前自住可选的户型主要分为独立屋、联排别墅、公寓三大类。通常来说,独立屋的面积要大于联排别墅,联排别墅大于公寓。价格方面也基本是独立屋最高,联排别墅次之,公寓相对价格最低。所以自住的购房者,需要按照自己的资金能力和居住需要首先确定购房准备功课的大方向。

自住房的另一个大方向是房屋位置。温西是温哥华传统意义上的核心地带,交通便利、学区等配套设施都最优秀,价格水平也最高。西温是依山傍海的别墅区,拥有大量超大面积、绝佳风景的豪宅,但交通不够便利,主要适于休闲人士。温东交通便利,房价也较为便宜,但配套设施和治安较差。列治文、本拿比整体来说房价最适中,可供选择的类型也最全面。其他每个区也都有自己的优、缺点。地点选择对于购房者来说需要考虑的问题更多、更复杂。很多时候不能做到面面俱到。比如一个家庭可能需要考虑上下班的通勤时间、子女的学校资源优劣、居住环境的优劣,甚至附近居民的种族、文化等。这一部分一般也是购房者最需要花时间考虑的问题。通常来讲,我们建议首先开家庭会议,列出需要的点,然后列出重要分级,再慢慢逐条研究。在这里购房者寻求专业人士的帮助将省去很多麻烦,但自身的参与和思考也绝对是必需的。

搞清了上面两个问题之后,购买自住房就进入第三个可能也是最后一个阶段,那就是实地看房。温哥华的地产市场通常在周六、周日下午两点到四点会有大量公开看房活动。地产经纪也可以通过预约的形式给购房者提供看房的机会。由于温哥华房地产市场的特殊性,房源之间的差别很大。尤其是独立屋,诸如朝向、景色、地形、房屋结构等方面在房源与房源之间差异巨大。只有实地看房,才可能确实地保证每一个细节都符合购房者的要求。

(4)温哥华房产交易流程及税费明细

在温哥华购买房产,通常第一步并不是搜索房源或选择目标地区,而是找一位(或几位)贷款经纪,确实地将购房者能够承担的房屋贷款做好审查和预批。这一步骤为购房提供了最基础的预算上限,同时也保证在后面的交易过程中不会被迫走回头路。

确定预算之后,下一步就是确定想要购买的挂牌房屋。上面已经提到,购房者可以选择承担风险自行挑选,也可以寻求专业地产经纪的帮助,这是每一位购房者的权利,温哥华并不强制要求购房者一定要有代理经纪。但需要提醒每一位购房者的是,温哥华的市场模式中,购房的佣金并不是从买家那里收取的,而是来自卖家。所以选择一位专业人士并没有任何的额外费用。

选定想要的房源之后,下一步就是出价,卖家如果接受报价并签字,买卖双方才算正式达成法定合约。签合约之后,首先需要买家向买家经纪公司的信托账户里存入押金,押金通常是房价的5%,需要在24小时或指定时间内交付。之后会有一两周或更长时间给买家准备贷款、请专业验屋师验屋、购买房屋保险、查询房产交易历史和核对房产证等。买卖双方也需要在这时准备好代理房产交易的律师或公证人。到买卖双方约定的交房日期时,买家将提前存入律师或公证人户头的房款转给买家律师或公证人,房产证件改名字也由律师或公证人完成。这些流程结束之后,买家领取钥匙完成一个完整的房产交易。

在温哥华购房,买家除了需要缴纳房款之外,还需要缴纳房产转让税、律师费、验屋费、保险费用等。房产转让税的收取方式是:房价的首20万加元收取1%,20万加元到200万加元的部分征收2%,200万加元到300万加元的部分征收3%,300万加元以上的部分征收5%。海外买家需要额外缴纳房价的20%作为惩罚性税收,目前这项政策自2016年8月至今一直存在。购买新房的买家需要额外缴纳5%的GST税,这项税务收取的具体限制可能需要咨询专业会计。

本文作者:

Philip Chen(陈兴),温哥华移民,曾任FX168金融研究院研究员,多年财经市场、政策分析经验,善于利用科学方法对房地产市场进行研究整理,对于政策、市场走向尤为敏感。精通英文、国语。熟悉整个大温地区市场。对于客户的每一个问题,必将提供一个实事求是、明确的答复。

Tiffany Chen(陈梦盈),温哥华早期移民,对加国房地产政策、市场动向、建筑潮流有着敏锐直觉。精通英文、粤语、国语、潮汕话。具有出色的协调沟通能力以及敏锐洞察力,工作态度积极、严谨,善于管理销售。熟悉整个大温地区市场特征、业务流程、专业技巧,根据市场变化及时调整对应政策。针对客户不同需求,必将为客户提供百分百满意的服务!

5.5 中东地区

5.5.1 埃及：房价急剧下跌

埃及的住房市场继续挣扎，到2019年第二季度，全国房地产指数暴跌21.51%，与2018年第二季度的同比增长12.17%形成鲜明对比。2019年第二季度的名义房价也同比下降14.15%。

尽管如此，人们普遍预计埃及的住房市场在未来几年会有所改善——高端建筑正在蓬勃发展以满足需求。为什么？从富有的埃及人的角度考虑情况，如果他住在国外，由于货币贬值，埃及的财产突然变得便宜得多。在2019年7月，平均汇率为每1美元兑16.61埃及镑，比决定浮动汇率前的8.88埃及镑的价值下降了47%。同时，埃及对住房的需求量很大，因为该国的人口每年增加250万。

但是，有些人认为供过于求，因为国家本身（通过军队）正在投资建设，特别是在埃及的新首都。

【埃及开罗房产数据】

表5.111　主要指标

指标	数值
价格收入比	12.46
抵押贷款占收入的百分比	178.51%
贷款承受能力指数	0.56
市中心租金价格比	16.07
出租价格比——中心以外	15.67
总租金收益率（市中心）	6.22%
总租金收益率（中心以外）	6.38%

表5.112　每月租金　　　　　　　　　　　　　　　　　　　　　　　　　单位：埃及镑

	每月租金均价	租金范围
市中心公寓（1间卧室）	3 420.29	2 000—6 000
市中心以外公寓（1间卧室）	1 918.85	1 000—3 000
市中心公寓（3间卧室）	6 348.81	4 000—10 000
市中心以外公寓（3间卧室）	4 041.33	2 000—6 500

表5.113　公寓价格　　　　　　　　　　　　　　　　　　　　　　　　　单位：埃及镑

	每平方米均价	单价范围
在市中心购买公寓	12 157.89	7 000—20 000
在中心以外购买公寓	7 064.52	4 000—12 000

表5.114　薪资和融资

	均　　值	范　　围
平均月净工资（税后）	3 857.64埃及镑	
抵押贷款利率/20年/固定利率	13.32%	10.0%—18.0%

数据来源：numbeo；数据更新时间：2019年12月。

表5.115　国家数据

人均国内生产总值	2 412.73美元
人口增长率	2.45%

数据来源：世界银行，2019年。

【非埃及居民购房政策】

根据1996年第230号法律，外国人可以在埃及购买财产。外国人不能购买超过两块不超过4 000平方米的房地产，其目的必须是让家庭成员住在该房地产中。购买必须得到部长理事会的批准，这大约需要两个月。如果注册，则该财产不能在五年内出售或出租。购买的款项必须通过其中一家公共商业银行以外汇形式带入埃及（尽管法律的这一规定没有得到执行）。

5.5.2　阿联酋：房地产价格进一步下跌

在迪拜，住宅房地产价格在截至2019年第二季度的一年中下降了6.86%，由于经济增长疲软，投资者情绪低迷以及住房供过于求，价格连续18个季度同比下跌。在最近一个季度，迪拜的房价环比下降3.26%。

迪拜的房地产市场一直是全球最动荡的市场之一。从2008年第三季度到2011年第三季度，迪拜是世界上最严重的房屋崩盘城市之一，房价暴跌了53%。

预计2019年迪拜的房价将保持低迷，这主要是由于供应量大。根据仲量联行的数据，2018年，迪拜的住宅总存量增加了约43 000套（2017年底约为491 000套），但阿布扎比市场仅增加了8 000套新住房（2017年底为251 000套）。

其他几个因素也影响了市场。2013年推出的《联邦抵押贷款上限》放慢了阿布扎比和迪拜的住宅价值升值步伐。此外，迪拜土地局最近将房地产登记费从2%翻了一番至4%，以抑制房地产需求。最后，增值税（VAT）的实施于2018年1月生效，这是另一个因素。5%的增值税仅适用于项目完成后三年以上出售的房屋。完成后三年内的销售增值税率为0%。

【阿联酋迪拜房产数据】

表5.116　主要指标

指标	数值
价格收入比	4.90
抵押贷款占收入的百分比	36.52%
贷款承受能力指数	2.74
市中心租金价格比	9.83
出租价格比——中心以外	9.34
总租金收益率（市中心）	10.17%
总租金收益率（中心以外）	10.70%

表5.117　每月租金　　　　　　　　　　　单位：迪拉姆

	每月租金均价	租金范围
市中心公寓（1间卧室）	5 611.25	4 000—7 500
市中心以外公寓（1间卧室）	3 737.81	2 800—5 000
市中心公寓（3间卧室）	11 256.14	8 000—15 000
市中心以外公寓（3间卧室）	7 667.74	5 000—10 000

表5.118　公寓价格　　　　　　　　　　　　　　　　　　　单位：迪拉姆

	每平方米均价	单价范围
在市中心购买公寓	12 660.63	8 000—17 222.26
在中心以外购买公寓	8 098.39	5 289.00—11 500.00

表5.119　薪资和融资

	均　值	范　围
平均月净工资（税后）	10 597.78迪拉姆	
抵押贷款利率/20年/固定利率	4.29%	3.0%—5.90%

数据来源：numbeo；数据更新时间：2019年12月。

表5.120　国家数据

人均国内生产总值	40 698.85美元
人口增长率	2.37%

数据来源：世界银行，2019年。

【非阿联酋居民购房政策】

现在允许外国公民在迪拜的指定区域购买永久产权的房地产。海湾合作委员会（GCC）国民可在阿联酋境内的任何地方拥有永久所有权。

可用于外国永久业权的一些开发项目包括Palm，卓美亚（Jumeirah），Emaar Towers，The Greens，International City等。在某些项目中，除了开放给外国永久业权的开发项目外，土地可以租赁长达99年。

通常，居留签证是发给财产所有人的，其适用范围包括其直系亲属。这些签证在拥有期间每三年更新一次。

5.6 拉美地区

5.6.1 墨西哥：2018年以来住房市场表现强劲

尽管经济不景气，墨西哥的住房市场仍在继续走强。全国房价指数在截至2019年第三季度的一年中增长了4.96%，是自2016年第二季度以来的最大增幅。按季度计算，最近一个季度的房价增长了1.21%。

十年来，墨西哥房地产市场几乎没有动静。2009年，房价上涨0.77%（经通货膨胀调整后），2010年下跌0.59%，2011年上涨2.37%，2012年下跌1.15%，2013年上涨0.39%，2014年上涨0.84%，2015年上涨4.36%，2016年上涨4.07%和2017年上涨0.73%，均已将通货膨胀因素调整后。2018年，房价强劲上涨4.32%。

奢侈品市场受到国内外需求的推动。国际房地产协会联合会（ICREA）表示，度假胜地的强劲需求推动了墨西哥的房地产市场。由于油价低迷和美元坚挺，美国和加拿大的买家在经历了连续数年的低迷后正重返墨西哥，这推高了房屋价格。

墨西哥不断增长的中产阶级继续推动房地产市场。据估计，该国的中产阶级几乎占总家庭的一半，为1 460万。他们预计将继续增长，预计到2030年将有380万家庭进入中产阶级家庭。

2019年11月，在通货膨胀放缓和经济增长缓慢的情况下，墨西哥央行（Banxico）将关键利率下调了25个基点，至7.5%，这是2019年以来连续第三次下调利率。受工业产值下滑和经济下滑的拖累，服务业疲软，墨西哥经济在2019年第三季度同比下降0.4%，此前2019年第二季度同比下降0.8%，在2019年第一季度同比增长1.2%。按季度计算，在上一季度公布了零增长之后，经济在2019年第三季度仅增长了0.1%。自2018年12月1日上任以来，新当选的总统安德烈斯·曼努埃尔·洛佩兹·奥夫拉多（Andres Manuel Lopez Obrador）一直警告投资者，宣誓要改变该国的"新自由主义"经济模式，并终止为墨西哥城投资130亿美元的新机场。该项目已经完成了三分之一，他突然取消该项目的决定引发了墨西哥金融资产的抛售。预计2019年经济仅增长0.4%，是2009年经济收缩5.3%以来的最低增幅。

【墨西哥房产数据】

表5.121 主要指标

指标	数值
价格收入比	15.37
抵押贷款占收入的百分比	194.19%
贷款承受能力指数	0.51
市中心租金价格比	17.10
出租价格比——中心以外	17.61
总租金收益率（市中心）	5.85%
总租金收益率（中心以外）	5.68%

表5.122 每月租金　　　　　　　　　　　　　　　单位：墨西哥元

	每月租金均价	租金范围
市中心公寓（1间卧室）	11 641.94	7 000—18 000
市中心以外公寓（1间卧室）	7 103.00	4 000—12 000
市中心公寓（3间卧室）	23 869.57	15 000—32 000
市中心以外公寓（3间卧室）	14 987.88	8 000—25 000

表5.123 公寓价格　　　　　　　　　　　　　　　单位：墨西哥元

	每平方米均价	单价范围
在市中心购买公寓	46 162.07	30 000—62 500
在中心以外购买公寓	29 400	15 000—40 000

表5.124 薪资和融资

	均　　值	范　　围
平均月净工资（税后）	12 292.32墨西哥元	
抵押贷款利率/20年/固定利率	11.3%	10.0%—13.0%

数据来源：numbeo；数据更新时间：2019年12月。

表5.125 国家数据

人均国内生产总值	8 910.33美元
人口增长率	1.12%

数据来源：世界银行，2019年。

【非墨西哥居民购房政策】

外国人在墨西哥的房地产购买是通过fideicomiso系统进行的。1917年的宪法宣布，墨西哥的所有土地均为"ejido"（公共）或仅由墨西哥国民拥有。Ejido的土地被分配给每个村庄，无法出售。

1973年，一项名为《外国投资法》的宪法修正案允许外国人在墨西哥任何地方购买房地产，但禁区除外，该禁区包括距国际边界100公里（64英里）或距海岸线50公里（32英里）的区域在涨潮时。在1993年，墨西哥修改了宪法，允许外国人通过fideicomiso在限制区内购买房地产。

5.6.2 智利：房价保持强劲

尽管过去两年开始征收房地产销售税，智利的住房市场仍然保持强劲。

大圣地亚哥地区的新公寓平均价格在2019年第三季度同比强劲增长6.5%，此前2019年第二季度同比增长9.05%，2019年第一季度同比增长5.04%，2018年第四季度同比增长6.94%和2018年第三季度同比增长4.29%。按季度计算，2019年第三季度房价小幅上涨0.24%。

征收19%的增值税对房地产公司等"惯常卖方"的房地产销售的影响正在减弱。智利建筑商会（CChC）的数据显示，2018年，全国新房销售同比增长5.5%，大圣地亚哥地区增长6.3%。

智利中央银行（Banco Central de Chile）的数据显示，由于采矿业前景改善，智利的经济在2019年第三季度同比增长3.3%，高于第二季度的1.9%和第一季度的1.6%的同比增长。智利是世界上最大的铜生产国。

然而，自2019年10月上旬开始的抗议活动已抑制了当年余下时间的前景，促使政府将其2019年经济增长预期从之前的2.4%下调至1.8%至2.2%的范围。地铁票价上涨引发了社会动荡，但也反映出人们对政府未能解决日益严重的不平等现象的不满情绪。因此，动乱估计使该国蒙受了30亿美元的损失和收入损失。

【智利圣地亚哥房产数据】

表5.126 主要指标

价格收入比	16.08
抵押贷款占收入的百分比	114.45%
贷款承受能力指数	0.87
市中心租金价格比	24.09
出租价格比——中心以外	26.10
总租金收益率(市中心)	4.15%
总租金收益率(中心以外)	3.83%

表5.127 每月租金　　　　　　　　　　　　单位：智利比索

	每月租金均价	租金范围
市中心公寓(1间卧室)	320 333.33	270 000—400 000
市中心以外公寓(1间卧室)	302 127.66	200 000—400 000
市中心公寓(3间卧室)	605 106.38	450 000—850 000
市中心以外公寓(3间卧室)	536 463.41	350 000—900 000

表5.128 公寓价格　　　　　　　　　　　　单位：智利比索

	每平方米均价	单价范围
在市中心购买公寓	1 721 148.15	1 100 000—2 350 000
在中心以外购买公寓	1 710 309.32	950 000—2 600 000

表5.129 薪资和融资

	均　值	范　围
平均月净工资(税后)	533 651.46 智利比索	
抵押贷款利率/20年/固定利率	3.76%	3.0%—5.0%

数据来源：numbeo；数据更新时间：2019年12月。

表5.130 国家数据

人均国内生产总值	15 346.45美元
人口增长率	0.77%

数据来源:世界银行,2019年。

【非智利居民购房政策】

任何个人或法人团体都可以在智利获得并拥有房地产,无论他们是否是居民。但是,对于位于该国边界附近的土地有一些限制。智利对财产权,包括对不动产的担保投资,具有强有力的法律保护。

FX168 投资地图篇

6.1 2019年FX168投资地图回顾

2018年末,根据对2019年经济及市场的判断,我们配置了一份较为谨慎保守的投资地图,分别挑选了四款ETF基金以及五款固定收益类债券基金,2019年的业绩表现如下:

表6.1 权益类投资标的2019年业绩表现

投资国家/行业	可选的投资标的（ETF基金）	上市交易所	2019年业绩
印度	iShares安硕核心标普BSE SENSEX 印度指数ETF 2836.HK	中国香港	12.67%
印度	该ETF投资印度孟买交易所的30间市值最大上市公司,经过筛选是印度股票投资的高流量交易工具,能够实现单一国家的多元化投资组合。近十年表现稳定,十年平均年化收益率为10.36%,享受到了印度高增长的红利。		
日本	领航富时日本指数ETF 3126.HK	中国香港	19.3%
日本	该基金寻求追踪富时日本指数的表现,分散投资于日本企业大型及中型股。		
以色列	iShare MSCI Israel ETF〈EIS〉	纽交所	18.4%
以色列	以色列在创新产品和服务的开发方面是领先的,该国交易所市值最高的两家公司所属行业分别是制药和软件服务。该基金投资于以色列大型和中型股。		
全球公共事业板块	iShare Global Utilities ETF〈JXI〉	纽交所	8.76%
全球公共事业板块	该基金分散投资超过十个国家的公共事业企业,公司类型包括但不仅限于电力、燃气和自来水公司。		

6　FX168投资地图篇

表6.2　固定收益类产品2019年业绩表现

可选的投资标的	基　金　点　评	2019年业绩
天利（卢森堡）—美元高收入债券基金	该基金各时长收益率均明显高于同组别基金，且收益率波动性较低。	15.41%
富达基金—亚洲高收益基金	该基金在晨星风格箱中被归于信用度低等、利率敏感度低等的分类，十年收益较高，但短期收益稍逊，因此适合更为长期的投资。	11.4%
联博—环球高收益基金I2 USD	从该基金目前的投资组合来看，其占比较大的投资基本为政府债券，包括美国政府债券和包括巴西、墨西哥和土耳其在内的新兴国家政府债券。在晨星风格箱中属于信用度低等、利率敏感度中等的类别。三年和五年评级为三星，十年评级为五星。	14.15%
JPM环球政府债券（美元对冲）	该基金主要投资于政府债券，目前的投资组合中占比最大的包括法国、美国、西班牙和日本政府发行的定息债券，风险较低，收益稳定。	7.6%
恒生香港债券基金	该债券基金多投资于香港机构发行的基金，也可投资政府债券，属于低风险基金，但收益率高于上述基金，且较为稳定。	9.69%

　　从表6.1、表6.2的数据来看，权益类标的的业绩没有跑赢MSCI基准指数，固定收益类产品表现不错。

6.2 2020年FX168金融投资地图

在金融投资品的选择方面,我们还是一如既往地推荐在中国香港上市的ETF基金。

ETF是一种开放式的投资基金,像其他上市可买卖证券一样,可于交易所进行买卖。ETF集合了简单、易于使用的产品优势,具有股票即日成交及高流动性的主要特点,并且像指数基金一样间接持有一篮子实物股票,或通过衍生工具追踪股票指数,以达到分散投资风险的目的。

中国香港ETF市场具有规模在区域内领先、监管规则符合国际标准、销售网络广泛、提供专业服务的中介机构众多等优势。另外,自2015年2月13日起,中国香港ETF全面免除印花税。

距离1999年中国香港第一只ETF基金在中国香港交易所上市,已经过去了20年。近年来,ETF发行商推出了杠杆及反向产品、主动型ETF、货币市场ETF等一系列的主题投资产品。随着产品类型的多样化,这一市场正在稳定地持续发展。每日成交额达50亿港元,占港股的每日成交额约8%,市场流动性极高。

2019年,在全球股市整体上涨的背景下,中国香港ETF基金提供了积极的回报率。在领先基金评级公司晨星(Morningstar)收录的至少运营一年的200只中国香港ETF基金中仅有15只收跌。收益最高的基金回报率超过10倍。

表6.3 2019年收益率最高的中国香港ETF基金

基 金 名 称	一年回报率（%）	三年年化回报率（%）
iShares 安硕纳斯达克 100 指数 ETF	1.26k	162.6
iShares 安硕核心 MSCI 台湾指数	1.26k	191.48
iShares DAX Index ETF	1.07k	128.67
iShares FTSE 100 Index ETF	1.04k	131.94
iShares 安硕核心韩国综合股价200指数 ETF	985.86	141.1
华夏 Direxion 纳斯达克 100 指数每日杠杆（2x）产品ETF	73.06	37.3
南方东英中国创业板指数 ETF	46.9	−2.17
db x-trackers MSCI 俄罗斯权重上限指数ETF	46.47	16.62
Horizons 沪深 300 指数 ETF	39.75	8.47
db x-trackers 沪深 300 指数 ETF	39.74	13.95

2020年中国香港ETF基金推荐

晨星评级

首先，对于股票型基金，晨星按照基金所投资的股票市值及行业分布，将其分为9类（风格箱）。类型分为大型、中型和小型，大型股票基金风险最低，小型风险最高。行业则分为价值型、均衡型和成长型，价值型风险最低，成长型风险最高。类型和行业排列组合（如大型价值型、中型均衡型等）而成这9类基金。

计算基金的风险调整后收益，在所在的类别中进行排位，排名在10%的获得五星，排在之后22.5%的获得四星，再之后35%、22.5%和10%的基金分别获得三星、二星和一星。评级衡量年限最短为三年，还包括五年和十年。

因此，总体来讲，晨星对基金的评级是对于基金在可同比前提下综合衡量风险收益在长期的评估。在此推荐五只晨星评级为四星或五星的ETF基金：

（1）db x-trackers MSCI 美国总回报净值指数 ETF

投资目标：德意志资产管理旗下的db x-trackers MSCI美国总回报净值指数ETF，提供在扣除费用及支出之前紧贴MSCI总回报净值指数的表现的投资回报。投资地区为美国，投资标的为股票型，MSCI美国总回报净值指数是一项公众持股量调整市值加权指数，为衡量美国股市表现而设计，针对的公司都是按净股息再投资后的总回报计算，其市值在美国可投资股票范围前85%之内的公司（在符合整体最小规模要求之下）。

表6.4 收益率

年份	2012	2013	2014	2015	2016	2017	2018	2019
收益率（%）	13.69	32.37	14.84	0.91	10.4	22.55	−5.37	31.8
跑赢类别（%）	1.2	1.13	4.09	2.65	0.87	1.42	1.68	4.04
跑赢指数（%）	−2.5	−0.79	1.58	0.05	−1.7	−0.14	−0.73	1

表6.5 晨星评级

评价时长	回报评价	风险评价	晨星评级
三年	高于平均	平均	★★★★
五年	高	平均	★★★★★
十年	高	平均	★★★★★
总体	高	平均	★★★★★

（2）iShares 安硕核心 MSCI 亚洲（日本除外）指数 ETF

投资目标：本基金乃 iShares 亚洲信托基金之成分基金，投资目标为提供在扣除费用及开支前，与 MSCI 综合亚洲（除日本）指数表现非常接近之投资回报。指数纳入亚洲（不包括日本）50 只最大股份而符合可交易标准之股份之表现。

表6.6 收益率

年份	2012	2013	2014	2015	2016	2017	2018	2019
收益率（%）	22.13	6.01	4.2	−8.41	5.79	42.38	−14.04	16.94
跑赢类别（%）	1.79	1.57	−0.36	−0.4	2.45	1.1	2.94	−1.81
跑赢指数（%）	0.02	2.9	−0.62	0.81	0.31	−0.51	0.2	−0.66

表6.7 晨星评级

评价时长	回报评价	风险评价	晨星评级
三年	平均	平均	★★★
五年	平均	平均	★★★

评价时长	回报评价	风险评价	晨星评级
十年	高于平均	平均	★★★★
总体	高于平均	平均	★★★★

（3）db x-trackers MSCI环球总回报净值指数ETF

投资目标：追踪MSCI总回报净值环球指数表现。该指数是公众持股量调整市值加权指数，所反映的是全球已发展市场中大型和中型资本公司的表现。所谓总回报净值指数，是指基于股息或分派额在扣除任何适用税项后再作投资来计算指数成分股的表现。

表6.8 收益率

年 份	2012	2013	2014	2015	2016	2017	2018	2019
收益率（%）	14.51	27.45	5.87	−0.28	6.13	23.39	−9.15	28.54
跑赢类别（%）	0.71	4.55	4.71	2.07	2.57	−0.87	2.89	5.32
跑赢指数（%）	−1.39	4.6	1.7	2.14	−1.77	−1.61	0.12	2.55

表6.9 晨星评级

评价时长	回报评价	风险评价	晨星评级
三年	高于平均	平均	★★★★
五年	高于平均	平均	★★★★
十年	高	低于平均	★★★★★
总体	高	平均	★★★★★

（4）Horizons MSC中国ETF

投资目标：追踪MSC中国指数，投资于业务主要位于中国的公司。

表6.10 收益率

年 份	2014	2015	2016	2017	2018	2019
收益率（%）	7.66	−7.32	1.35	54.12	−17.77	22.14

(续表)

年份	2014	2015	2016	2017	2018	2019
跑赢类别（%）	0.35	−2.42	3.63	8.98	2.06	−1.76
跑赢指数（%）	−0.32	0.56	0.42	−1.22	0.98	−0.72

表6.11　晨星评级

评价时长	回报评价	风险评价	晨星评级
三年	高于平均	高于平均	★★★★
五年	高于平均	平均	★★★★
十年	—	—	未评级
总体	高于平均	平均	★★★★

（5）iShares安硕纳斯达克100指数ETF

投资目标：旨在提供扣除费用及开支之前与纳斯达克100指数表现非常接近的投资回报。

表6.12　收益率

年份	2017	2018	2019
收益率（%）	34.67	−2.96	1 287.59
跑赢类别（%）	13.54	4.1	1 259.83
跑赢指数（%）	11.97	1.68	1 256.8

表6.13　晨星评级

评价时长	回报评价	风险评价	晨星评级
三年	高	高	★★★★★
五年	—	—	未评级
十年	—	—	未评级
总体	高	高	★★★★★

另外，鉴于黄金市场的投资价值，我们特别推荐在中国香港市场上市的价值黄金ETF。

投资目标：本基金旨在提供与伦敦黄金市场定价有限公司所公布的以美元报价的每盎司黄金早盘（伦敦时间）定盘价非常接近的投资回报（未扣除费用及开支）。本信托持有实金并且库存在香港。

表6.14 收益率

年 份	2017	2018	2019
收益率(%)	11.66	−2.06	17.45
跑赢类别(%)	−6.62	2.07	−2.94
跑赢指数(%)	—	—	—

6.3 2020年FX168房产投资地图

根据标准普尔的数据,在不考虑通货膨胀因素的情况下,美国房屋价格现在比2007年的最高水平高出15%。在英国,尽管过去三年来,住房受到英国退欧不确定性的打击,价格仍比2008年上涨了21%。与此同时,在澳大利亚、加拿大和新西兰,住房在2009年初几乎没有下跌,后来又疯狂上涨:如今与2009年相比平均增长了40%。

那么,在此背景下,2020年,全球房产市场该如何选择投资标的? 首先,我们先来看看亚洲市场,如表6.15所示。

表6.15 亚洲房产市场

国家城市	价格收入比	抵押贷款占收入的百分比(%)	贷款承受能力指数	市中心租金价格比	市中心以外租金价格比	总租金收益率(市中心)(%)	总租金收益率(中心以外)(%)	抵押贷款利率/20年/固定利率(%)	人口增长率(%)
日本东京	14.16	81.98	1.22	38.8	37.36	2.58	2.68	1.0—2.0	−0.21
新加坡	22.37	142.95	0.7	42.37	37.95	2.36	2.64	2.0—4.0	1.82
韩国首尔	22.97	160.73	0.62	71.4	56.42	1.40	1.77	3.0—4.5	0.48
马来西亚吉隆坡	10.89	83.21	1.2	25.55	23.33	3.91	4.29	4.0—5.7	1.37
柬埔寨金边	33.74	354.96	0.28	17.6	15.29	5.68	6.54	6.0—15.0	1.52
印度孟买	42.73	470.19	0.21	44.1	36.68	2.27	2.73	8.25—11.0	1.17

(续表)

国家城市	价格收入比	抵押贷款占收入的百分比(%)	贷款承受能力指数	市中心租金价格比	市中心以外租金价格比	总租金收益率（市中心）(%)	总租金收益率（中心以外）(%)	抵押贷款利率/20年/固定利率(%)	人口增长率(%)
泰国曼谷	27.24	225.69	0.44	28.42	28.52	3.52	3.54	3.5—7.75	0.30
菲律宾马尼拉	24.38	244.75	0.41	15.22	23.38	6.57	4.28	7.5—8.5	1.57

数据来源：numbeo；更新时间：2019年12月。

仔细分析表6.15，我们发现如下几点：

第一，从租金收益率与贷款利率差的数据比较来看，日本东京的利差是正数，新加坡、马来西亚吉隆坡接近平衡，其他城市均为负值，印度孟买的利差最大。也就是说，除了东京以外的其他城市，其每月租金收入无法覆盖每月还款额。

第二，从贷款承受能力指数来看，日本东京的承受能力最强，印度孟买的最弱。这反映了本地居民的购房能力，也可以认为是本地的接盘能力。

第三，如果单独看租金收益率，菲律宾马尼拉、柬埔寨金边均处于较高水平，但是菲律宾马尼拉的贷款承受能力高于柬埔寨金边，因此，菲律宾马尼拉的投资价值高于柬埔寨金边。同时，如果选择在菲律宾买房，因为贷款利率高企，避免选择在当地贷款。

综上，在亚洲市场，比较可以选择的投资标的有日本东京、马来西亚吉隆坡、菲律宾马尼拉。新加坡因为有极高的海外买家税，暂剔除。

接下来，我们重点来看华人较多的城市以及提供移民政策的国家城市的房产市场（见表6.16）：

表6.16 华人较多、提供移民政策的国家城市的房产市场

国家城市	价格收入比	抵押贷款占收入的百分比(%)	贷款承受能力指数	市中心租金价格比	市中心以外租金价格比	总租金收益率（市中心）(%)	总租金收益率（中心以外）(%)	抵押贷款利率/20年/固定利率(%)	人口增长率(%)
澳大利亚悉尼	11.34	81.55	1.23	25.13	22.87	3.98	4.37	3.15—4.5	1.03
新西兰惠灵顿	6.29	44.55	2.02	16.89	15.04	5.92	6.65	4.0—6.0	0.79
英国伦敦	22.02	150.52	0.66	34.64	27.36	2.89	3.65	2.25—5.0	0.52
德国柏林	10.59	63.38	1.58	29.69	26.5	3.37	3.77	1.4—2.0	−0.16

（续表）

国家城市	价格收入比	抵押贷款占收入的百分比(%)	贷款承受能力指数	市中心租金价格比	市中心以外租金价格比	总租金收益率（市中心）(%)	总租金收益率（中心以外）(%)	抵押贷款利率/20年/固定利率(%)	人口增长率(%)
葡萄牙里斯本	17.97	109.52	0.91	21.34	17.42	4.69	5.74	1.25—3.0	0.04
西班牙马德里	12.54	77.4	1.29	25.99	20.43	3.85	4.89	1.90—2.90	0.04
希腊雅典	11.08	86.02	1.16	22.13	23.48	4.52	4.26	3.5—6.0	−0.06
土耳其伊斯坦布尔	11.34	235.94	0.42	20.66	17.53	4.84	5.70	15.0—25.0	0.52
马耳他瓦莱塔	13.81	104.43	0.96	18.86	12.01	5.3	8.32	3.0—8.0	0.26
美国纽约	11.04	81.08	1.22	20.29	16.99	4.93	5.88	3.5—4.5	0.81
加拿大温哥华	14.58	104.01	0.96	27.62	27.22	3.62	3.67	3.05—4.5	0.73
阿联酋迪拜	4.90	36.52	2.74	9.83	9.34	10.17	10.70	3.0—5.9	2.37

数据来源：numbeo；更新时间：2019年12月。

从表6.16可以看出，土耳其伊斯坦布尔的房产投资情况不是很理想，阿联酋迪拜的状况最优，但是需考虑到中东的局势问题，宜保持长期关注，逢低入手。

投资重点可关注新西兰惠灵顿、葡萄牙里斯本与西班牙马德里，其他城市的情况均较为均衡，暂时可以保持观望。

7

疫情下的全球投资市场

2020年,一场突如其来的疫情,快速席卷全球,改变了我们的生活,也给全球投资市场带来了巨大的冲击。

下面,我们将重点解析疫情下的主要投资市场:美股、美元、黄金、原油及全球房产市场。

7.1 美股

道琼斯指数从2020年2月21日开始连续下跌,从28 992.41点到3月23日一路跌至18 591.93点,随后反弹,4月29日升至24 633.86点。同一时期内,标普500指数从2月20日的3 373.23点到3月23日跌至2 237.40点,4月29日反弹至2 939.51点;纳斯达克指数从2月19日的9 817.18点到3月23日跌至6 860.67点,5月11日反弹至9 192.34点。

短短两个月的时间内,美国主要股指的波动性惊人,涨跌幅度均超过了30%。其间由于单日涨/跌幅过大,发生了数次史上罕见的熔断。金融危机时美股跌至熊市用了200天,这次仅用了20天,4月的涨幅却又创下了数十年来少有的佳绩。

如此异常的波动从根本上看是源自新冠疫情的扩散。2020年3月11日世卫组织正式宣布COVID-19病毒疫情为全球大流行病。美国也成为世界上新冠疫情最为严重的国家。随着欧美及其他国家或地区为控制疫情而实施封锁政策,对于经济的担忧由供应链危机转为全球性经济衰退。

这一第二次世界大战以来最为严峻的全球性危机导致以美股为首的全球股市大跌。VIX恐慌指数飙升至接近2008年金融危机时的水平。且当时的情况是一切资产几乎都遭到了投资者的无差别抛售,黄金之类的避险资产也不例外。

与此同时,美联储果断"出手"救市,2020年3月3日紧急降息,3月15日直接降息到零,还启动了万亿美元的量化宽松政策,并且破天荒地开始购买垃圾债券。另一方面,美国政府也出台了空前规模的财政支持政策。

值得注意的是,美国股市反映的是投资者对于企业未来收益

数据来源：TradingView。

图7.1　2020年以来道琼斯指数日线图（截至2020年5月12日）

表现的预期，所以尽管企业财报已经纷纷显示出受到疫情打击，一连串刷新历史纪录的数据也体现出美国乃至全球经济现状有多么糟糕，但疫情缓解、主要国家开始放松封锁，再加上美联储和美国政府史无前例的联合刺激政策，致使美国股市从低谷极速反弹。

而对于美国股市的后续走势，专家们的预期也不尽相同。

一方认为，3月份的大跌实际上为投资者创造了买入的好时机。他们认为疫情所造成的经济损伤是暂时的，一旦经济随着各国政府解除封锁，恢复正常，人们继续生产和消费，股市也必然回归活力。

同时美联储为市场注入了巨额的流动性，加上政府实施的大力刺激政策，分析认为这次的政策相比金融危机时要及时得多，且力度也更大，而这些都将在一段时间内持续推升股市。

Brooks Macdonald资产管理公司最近就将国际股票评级为增持，其副首席投资官Edward Park说："当我们看到主要市场在3月份下跌，会发现一些价值型股票的价格开始具有吸引力。新冠疫情造成的打击巨大，但可能是短期的，不会影响长期的经济增长。所以我们预期本季度糟糕的公司和经济数据过后，未来会稍显乐观，尤其是在政府和央行实施了大力的财政和货币政策的情况下。"

Sethi Financial的罗伯·摩根（Rob Morgan）指出："历史上来看，下一轮牛市通常发生在衰退之中，我们现在可能经历两个月的经济衰退，然后会恢复，而标普500指数可能已经进入下一轮牛市。"截至2020年5月12日，标普500指数较3月23日的低位上涨了31.38%。

但也正因为美联储这波行动的"火力"猛烈，加上美股回升过快，一些业界权威认为这并非以往十几年一次的"抄底良机"。巴菲特在最近的伯克希尔·哈撒韦股东大会中说："美联储采取行动之前有一段时间,我们开始有一些买入机会,但并不吸引人。在美联储采取行动之后,其中有许多企业坦率地说能够以我们无法给出的条件在公开市场上获得资金。"

也就是说,巴菲特这次并没有按照他的名言——"当别人贪婪时恐惧,当别人恐惧时贪婪"——那样做,而是在此次危机中仍坐拥大笔现金,特别是在他出售了自己的航空公司股票之后。他显然认为目前的美股估值并不吸引人,而这是否代表他认为股市会再次走低?

实际上,市场上有不少投资者都正持有类似的谨慎态度。安联(Allianz)首席经济顾问、彭博观点专栏作家穆罕默德·埃里安(Mohamed El-Erian)最近就表示:"我不太放心投注太多,我不太放心押注'紧急援助',我不太放心美联储总会介入的概念以及基于此对股票的买入。我们讨论的不再是丧失生产力的僵尸企业,我们讨论的是'僵尸市场',这个市场不再能有效运作资本。所以我想我们必须小心。我理解有人这些年来对运行如此好的股市所吸引,但我对此感到不适。"

不少分析都指出市场再次探底并非不可能。CNBC的报道称,数据显示过去30天里有1万亿美元逃出资本市场套现。投资研究公司Leuthold Group首席投资策略师James Paulsen说:"市场上现在确实没有多少买家,这极不寻常,正像2009年3月份时股市触底,那时市场也没有买家。我认为下一阶段将是随着信心重回市场,买家会增多,但现在还没到那个阶段。"

更为悲观的预期甚至认为近期内还会有股市的"第二波"暴跌。美国知名金融分析师和评论员Gary Shilling近期表示:"这看起来像是熊市中反弹,类似于1929—1930年的大萧条时期。随着全球深度经济衰退,股市可能还有30%—40%的跌幅,直至2021年。""目前为止实施以及将来有可能加码的财政刺激政策不太可能弥补新冠疫情造成的巨大破坏。"

目前多数分析都认为全球经济的复苏会是"U"形,而非最初预期的"V"形。同时各国解除封锁后民众如何适应——他们是否会迅速回到购物中心和购物街,他们是否会放心外出就餐,都无法确定。更重要的是股市以及全球经济之所以面临危机的罪魁祸首——新冠疫情。只要疫苗及特效药没有成功研制出来,全人类都要面临这一风险。有专家提醒说如果出现第二波疫情可能让市场受到"惊吓"。

在短期或中期我们需要关注的是,糟糕的经济数据是否能持续好转,疫情是否不会再次复发。

现在唯一可以确定的是,在如此大的不确定性中,美股的波动性必将保持较高水平,这也意味着风险居高不下。

当然风险中也存在着机遇。美联储的超级宽松货币政策意味着美元的下跌,而Sethi Financial的罗伯·摩根称:"美元的下跌也可以帮助(美股)大盘股,同时材料能源板块正被低估,而公用事业、电信、医疗等防御型板块具有收益保障,这些将是我们未来专注的行业。"

另外,疫情也为可见的未来带来新的趋势。例如,社会交流的虚拟化以及需要追踪定位疑似感染者之类的新需求无疑将促进科技行业,而人们对公共卫生相关行业也必然会投入更多的关注。

总之,基本可以认为此次新冠疫情危机中最糟糕的部分已经过去,但美股风险尚存——因为美国还没有走出经济衰退,对抗新冠病毒最有力的"武器"也还没研制出来;同时也机遇尚存——无论是那些价格被压低的价值型股票,还是在新趋势中势必崛起的行业和个股。

7.2 美元指数

疫情的爆发虽然给全球金融市场带来了极大的冲击，但我们发现，整个金融市场的走势变化其实都有一条主线，那就是美元走势。可以这么说，由于美元的国际结算地位，其流动性的表现就会直接影响各主要资产板块的走势。

在疫情爆发时，金融市场全线下跌，加上主要交易所为了控制风险，已经开始要求提高保证金，因此机构方面需要大量的资金来填补保证金缺口，这一方面将市场大量流动性消耗掉，另一方面也造成了传统避险资产黄金的下跌。而普通民众方面，出于对失业和收入减少的忧虑，也在不停地卖出股票等资产来套现，并把美元牢牢攥在手中，从而应对生活需求。同时还要考虑的一点是，美元毕竟是全球流通货币，结合美国经济面的相对强势，美元在突发情况下是具备避险价值的。因此在崩盘风险下，大量的海外机构以及个人也对美元有着极高的需求，这就导致流动性急剧缩减，换言之就是市场中流通的美元数量严重不足。美元物以稀为贵，就进一步推高了美元的汇率，令美股、原油以及黄金的投资成本一起变高了，资产价格自然就会受到打压。

3月以来，美联储实施了史无前例的货币刺激政策，以应对经济下行以及流动性危机所引发的资产抛售，"零利率+无限量化宽松（QE）"的货币政策，短短两个月时间就扩表两万多亿美元。同时，美联储联合全球五大央行采取协调行动，利用现有货币互换额度为美元流动性提供支持，各央行一致同意将货币互换协议价格下调25个基点。另外，美联储与9家中央银行建立了临时的美元流动性互换安排，美联储与澳大利亚、巴西、韩国、墨西哥、新加坡和瑞典各自达成不超过600亿美元的新互换安排，与丹麦、挪威和新西兰各

数据来源：FX168。

图7.2 2020年美元指数日线图（截至5月12日）

自达成300亿美元的安排。这使得市场的流动性已经得到明显的改善，不仅令金融市场重归稳定，美国股市大幅反弹，同时美元指数也重归100美元关口附近。

但整体来看，由于疫情的影响在短时间内恐怕很难消散，因此美元依然会受到投资者和企业的争抢，美元融资压力在一定时间里可能依然沉重。但部分分析师以及越来越多的投机客开始相信，美联储的干预措施可能最终逆转美元两年来的升值趋势，这令100关口对于美元指数而言是个巨大的阻力，每次突破后都会遭遇空头的大量围剿。

另一方面，有消息称，美国2021年1月份联邦基金利率期货报价显示，市场预期美联储有实施负利率的可能性。受此影响，美元指数在未来几个月内进一步走低的风险正在攀升，除非疫情出现大范围的二次爆发。尽管如此，基金经理、分析师都表示美联储实施负利率的可能性几乎没有，且美联储主席鲍威尔等也反驳了负利率的可能性。对此，R.W. Pressprich & Co. 政府债券部门负责人Larry Milstein看来，可能是因为一些投资者认为美联储已经没有更多杠杆可用了。

摩根大通资产管理公司首席全球策略师David Kelly此前就曾认为，美联储将利率降为负值将毫无意义，而且在美国实施庞大财政刺激和美联储购债政策时，负利率政策完全没有必要。美联储主席鲍威尔也于4月底明确表示，现阶段美联储除了观望之外不会有更多行动。市场普遍预计鲍威尔将继续坚持不会实施负利率的立场。

然而，从历史数据看，以美联储四轮量化宽松为例，美元在量化宽松初期往往会录得上涨，但是随后几个月将会有所走低。从政策目的和刺激手段来看，美联储当前的情况和QE1类似，这意味着随着流动性危机缓解，美元可能迎来较大幅度的回调。

7.3 黄金市场

在前期进行黄金预测模型中针对黄金未来走势影响因素分析中,我们主要考虑的角度是黄金基于避险的属性和通胀的属性,其中有以避险属性为主。我们分析的主要角度是全球经济和地缘政治的不确定性等会为黄金市场注入上涨活力。而开局居然是一个席卷全球的疫情,确实是在我们的分析框架之内,又在我们的预料之外的,而在疫情下各国央行的超级量化宽松政策,将为黄金市场未来价格上涨提供原动力。因此我们在模型研究中把2020年定义为新一波黄金价格上涨的元年,而且在我们的模型中,我们认为在避险需求、保值增值等因素的作用下,在超级放水的情况下,未来黄金价格大概率会创出历史新高。

从价格走势角度来说,2020年度前四个月黄金市场经历了两次上涨和一次宽幅震荡,大概的时间周期是1月份和4月份黄金市场快速上涨,一月份价格从开盘的1 517.40美元/盎司上涨到1 588.12美元/盎司,涨幅为4.6%;四月份黄金开盘为1 575.70美元/盎司上涨到1 686.00美元/盎司,涨幅为6.9%,并且在盘中刷新2012年11月以来新高,至1 747.36美元/盎司;2月份和3月份行情基本维持一个宽幅震荡格局。

2020年度黄金价格形成的原因深受疫情的影响。1月份基本上疫情影响较小,黄金维持2019年的上涨行情,甚至在2020年2月份早期,疫情主要发生在中国境内的情况下,国际金价依旧维持在一个上涨行情中,但是明显的黄金价格波动幅度开始增大,进入2月下旬,疫情开始在全球蔓延,市场开始进入大幅波动阶段,而权益市场在避险作用下流动性快速出现枯竭。为了补充流动性,比较容易变现的黄金资产在市场中遭遇大量抛售,从而形成3月份

数据来源：FX168财经网。

图7.3　现货黄金2020年日线图（截至2020年5月9日）

的黄金价格大幅下跌，在短短9个交易日，黄金价格从最高的1 703.09美元/盎司下跌到最低时的1 451.10美元/盎司，下跌幅度高达14.80%。之后美联储在3月15日大幅度降息100个基点，将美国的利率一举下调到0—0.25的区间，并且美联储和全球其他国家或地区央行一起开始前所未有的扩表行动。3月16日美联储推出7 000亿美元的QE计划；3月17日开始商业票据融资机制，即所谓的CPFF；3月18日推出货币市场共同基金流动性工具，即所谓的MMLF；3月19日宣布联合澳大利亚储备银行、巴西央行、丹麦国家银行等9家央行成立临时美元流动性安排，3月20日又开始启动一级交易商信贷便利机制，即所谓的PDCF。在这个过程中市场流动性快速缓解，而黄金作为避险属性也快速获得交易者配置，在四月份价格快速上涨并且一举创出2012年11月以来的新高。

对于未来黄金价格的走势，我们认为在当前全球量化宽松的背景下，为了缓解疫情对经济的打击，在美国几乎无限量的购买资产这个背景下，当前黄金价格的上涨在中长期来看仅仅是一轮新价格启动的起始阶段，未来黄金价格就像美联储的无限量宽松一样，黄金价格上行将会有无限量想象空间。

7.4 原油市场

2020年3月7日的前一日以沙特为首的欧佩克组织与俄罗斯等盟国的减产谈判六年来首次没有达成任何协议，作为昔日的盟友，沙特和俄罗斯这两大产油国突然就撕破脸，不仅双双撕毁了之前的减产协议，还迅速拉开了原油大战的帷幕。沙特降价加增产的双重打击，直接令国际油价在3月9日暴跌30%，创下1991年美国发动伊拉克战争以来的最大单日跌幅。如果我们仔细回想一下，其实美国股市的这轮大崩盘也正是从3月9日油价开始暴跌后全面升级的，因为正式从那天开始，美国股市在短短10天里就经历了历史上4次熔断，而美国股市历史上一共才出现了5次熔断。

这次的原油大战局势可谓是沙特、俄罗斯和美国三国各有图谋。沙特和俄罗斯表面对抗，虽然心没往一处想，但劲却往一处使，目的就是拉美国下水，能击垮页岩油自然是完美解决，但若不能，至少也要让美国一起减产，这样就能拖住美国能源行业的扩张步伐，可以说是上演了一出漂亮的"苦肉计"。

不过，就在美国原油行业危在旦夕之际，沙特方面犯下了一个错误。而这个错误很有可能会导致沙特最终功亏一篑。沙特在选择发动原油大战的时机方面是准确的，那就是疫情爆发的时候打响原油价格战，因为如果不是有这种历史级别的原油需求大降，即便沙特和俄罗斯大打价格战，油价的跌幅也不足以拖美国一起减产。但沙特漏算了库存问题。由于原油大战开启后，产量攀升，全球原油储存空间有限，再不减产，很快全世界就没地方储存原油了。这也就解释了，为什么即便俄罗斯一直希望美国主动承诺减产，但就在美国快撑不下去的时候，突然沙特和俄罗斯就达成了石油输出国组织（OPEC）历史上最大规模的减产协议，从2020年5月1日开始

数据来源：FX168。

图7.4 2020年WTI原油日线图（截至5月12日）（单位：美元/桶）

每日减产970万桶，7月1日开始减产幅度降至每日800万桶，从2021年1月1日开始减产幅度进一步降至每日600万桶。

同时也正是库存问题的存在，导致美国WTI原油5月期货合约出现了历史性的负油价。在美国原油主要交割地库欣地区的库存空间即将耗尽的紧张局势下，许多交易员被迫平掉了5月合约多头仓位，这样抛售一边倒的情况下，空头自然就大开杀戒，出现油价跌出负37美元的极端情况。

不过在此之后，原油基本面情况开始改善，主要得益于负油价带来的强烈冲击导致主要产油国纷纷采取减产行动。随着OPEC减产行动的实施，各非OPEC产油国也开始配合减产，同时美国的原油产量也因油价走低引发了原油企业的被迫减产。市场普遍预计，美国原油产量在2020年年底之前将减少每日200万至300万桶。

值得注意的是，美国油服公司贝克休斯（Baker Hughes）5月8日公布的数据显示，美国当周石油活跃钻井数减少33座至292座；美国石油和天然气活跃钻井总数减少34座至374座；美国当周天然气活跃钻井数减少1座至80座。在新冠疫情导致油价暴跌后，美国钻井公司已经将石油和天然气钻井数量削减至历史最低水平。美国天然气钻井数跌至有记录以来的最低水平，美国石油钻井数则跌至11年新低。

摩根士丹利的分析师在一份研究报告中就表示："最大的供需失衡可能已经过去。从现在开始，需求可能会缓慢改善，供应方面的调整可能会加快步伐。这种再平衡可能会持续一段时间，有起有伏，但它仍将是一种再平衡。"这反映出当前投资者对原油市场的一种积极看法。

受投资情绪的改善和基本面的逐步稳定，原油价格已经从4月下旬触及的低位强势反弹，美国原油一度逼近30美元/桶，布伦特原油则一度站上32美元/桶。整体而言，只要疫情不出现进一步的恶化，如果以沙特为首的OPEC组织能够继续落实减产行动，同时其他产油国也适度配合减产，随着需求的逐步恢复，布伦特原油有望在2020年年底重回50美元/桶上方。

7.5 全球房产市场

随着疫情在全球加速扩散,许多国家关闭边境并限制旅行,全球房地产市场几乎陷入停顿。

首先,我们来看看几个主要国家或地区房产市场的最新统计数据:

- **中国**

根据中国国家统计局的数据,2020年1—3月份,商品房销售面积21 978万平方米,同比下降26.3%。其中,住宅销售面积下降25.9%,办公楼销售面积下降36.2%,商业营业用房销售面积下降35.1%。商品房销售额20 365亿元,同比下降24.7%。其中,住宅销售额下降22.8%,办公楼销售额下降36.8%,商业营业用房销售额下降39.8%。

3月份,初步测算,4个一线城市新建商品住宅销售价格环比由上月持平转为上涨0.2%,但涨幅比1月份回落0.2个百分点。其中,北京持平,上海和深圳分别上涨0.1%和0.5%,广州下降0.5%。二手住宅销售价格环比上涨0.5%,涨幅比上月扩大0.3个百分点,与1月份相同。其中,北京、上海和深圳分别上涨0.2%、0.3%和1.6%,广州下降0.2%。

- **加拿大**

大温地产局(REBGV)发布统计称,2020年4月大温的房地产市场共成交住宅房屋1 109套,比上年同期的1 829套下降了39.4%,比2020年3月的成交房屋2 524套降幅高达56.1%。

多重挂牌系统(MLS®)2020年4月新上市的待售独立屋,联排住宅和公寓有2 313套,与2019年4月上市的5 742套房屋相比减少了59.7%,与2020年3月的4 436套房屋上市相比减少了47.9%。

147

2020年4月的销售挂牌比率为11.8%。按物业类型分别计算,独立屋的比例为10%,联排住宅的比例为14.7%,公寓的比例为12.4%。

温哥华都会区所有住宅物业的MLS®房屋价格指数综合基准价格为每套1 036 000加元。这比2019年4月增加了2.5%,与2020年3月相比增加0.2%。

独立屋基准价:1 462 100加元(3月为1 450 700加元)。

联排屋基准价:796 800加元(3月为791 800加元)。

公寓基准价:685 500加元(3月为687 000加元)。

大多伦多地产局(TREB)2020年4月份市场报告:房地产市场行情随着疫情紧急令骤然降温,无论是成交量,还是上市均量都大幅降低2/3,但成交价格与上年同期基本持平。

大多伦多地区4月份MLS®系统报告了2 975笔住宅交易,与2019年4月同比下降67%,与2020年3月环比也下降66.2%;新增上市量6 174套,同比上年下降64.1%。但是GTA地区的房屋价格(所有类型),仍与2019年同期几乎持平,为821 392加元,且与2019年同期平均价格820 373加元相比,小幅上升了0.1%,与3月份902 680加元的均价相比,环比下降9.1%。4月的每日销售额保持在相对稳定的范围内,平均每天130套。

根据大多伦多地产局(TREB)的数据,大多伦多地区独立屋2019年3月的均价是110.7万加元,到4月份下降到98.4万加元,下降了12.3万加元。

- 美国

全美房地产中介协会(National Association of Realtors, NAR)数据显示,2020年3月份全美房屋交易按月跌了8.5%,但房价中位数反而按年增长8%,至28万美元。NAR数据显示,3月底有150万间待售房屋,较上年同期下跌了10.2%。

- 英国

根据英国银行Nationwide的房价统计数据,2020年4月(整个月都处在封锁期),英国房价对比2020年3月上涨了0.7%,对比2019年同期上涨了3.7%。3.7%的年增长率为英国近26个月以来的最高值,显示英国房价近两年基本处于平稳状态。

- 澳大利亚

澳房地产研究机构Corelogic的统计数据显示,2020年4月份澳大利亚房价环比上涨0.3%,低于3月份的0.7%,为2019年6月份以来的最低涨幅。随着上市房源数量大幅下降,4月份的房地产销售额下降了40%。悉尼房价保持稳定,4月份环比上涨0.4%,同比上涨14.3%。4月墨尔本房地产市场环比下跌0.3%,同比上涨12.4%。

- 日本

根据日本不动产流通机构的统计,2020年3月三大都市圈二手公寓的价格基本平缓。中部圈环比上涨2.3%,近畿圈环比上涨0.1%,首都圈环比下跌2%。其中东京23区的房价表现坚挺,环比小幅上涨0.1%,同比上涨3.4%。

从以上数据可以看出,受疫情的影响,各个国家或地区的房产交易量下降明显,但是住宅类房价却基本保持稳定。

交易量的下降主要源于疫情的短期效应。因为人们将在艰难时期暂时不再购买奢侈品和高价商品。由于对不久的将来缺乏信心,加上业务关闭持续时间的不确定性,潜在的买家可能会拭目以待,从而导致交易量下降。这些对于核心区位资产的影响基本趋于短期,且成熟市场相较于新兴市场将恢复更快。

同时,经过了2008年次贷危机之后,银行有更多的经验应对失业、经济衰退带来的房地产信贷、信用卡信贷违约。为了应对疫情对经济的影响,美国政府实施了抵押贷款减免措施,推出"房贷延期支付计划"(Mortgage forbearance program),即只要贷款人是从政府支持的房贷(Government-backed mortgage)机构贷款,就可以延期至少90天还款,甚至可以延期1年还款。在最新公布的2020年第一季度财报中,华尔街大行纷纷未雨绸缪调升坏账拨备率。与此同时,摩根大通还提高了新房贷标准,宣布从2020年4月14日起,房贷申请人需要满足两个条件:第一,申请人的信用等级分超过700分;第二,申请人有能力缴纳总房价20%的首付,此前仅为10%左右。

但疫情爆发的长期影响将更为深远,因为它将影响消费者的生活方式,导致人们工作、购物和生活方式的转变,从而改变相关的房地产要求。例如,由于在迁徙限制期间培养了灵活而偏远的工作文化,预计办公室型企业的规模将缩小。同时,由于消费者不断变化的购买方式,零售业,尤其是购物中心的建筑面积将相应减少。随着越来越多的消费者在日常生活中依赖智能设备,对无缝响应式服务和产品的需求正在增长。结果,将来与人类接触较少的电子商务产品和送货上门服务将会蓬勃发展。

下面,我们来看看高力国际(Colliers International,全球顶尖的房地产服务和咨询公司之一)2020年2月在中国市场的一个调研,或许可以找到未来的投资方向。

高力国际于2020年2月在中国进行了一次大规模的调研,这次调研对象共包括超700名房东、租户、零售商、数据中心运营商、物流供应商和投资者,涉及一线城市和新兴城市。

从调研结果可以看到如下趋势:

(1)写字楼租赁市场的空置率面临上升压力

该调研发现,超过90%的写字楼租户在2020年没有扩租意向。

(2)零售商业短期受创严重

零售层面,疫情对餐饮、零售、娱乐等业态带来巨大影响,预计大型购物中心空置率将有所提高,平均租金面临下调。且随着疫情爆发,零售物业对运营管理的标准也相应提高,导致运营成本有所增加。

(3)物流和数据中心业态可能会出现强烈的租赁需求

调查显示,随着网购和远程办公在中国得到更广泛的认可,电商和物流运营商获得更大的客户基础,包括以往不熟悉电子商务的老年人。而且,相关的用户习惯养成不可逆转。

(4)健康不动产的关注度提高

在疫情恐慌刺激下,提升人们对健康不动产(例如对老年公寓等业态)的需求更为关注。因疫情危机带来的健康恐慌,可能使更多人意识到,居住在大城市郊区低密度、高质量的老年公寓里,远离人口拥挤,可能会更加成为老年人的健康生活选择。

对投资者来说,要想在疫情之后抄底全球房产市场,重要的不仅仅是要看疫情后当地市场的短期变化,更要拉长时间维度,看看当地市场是否已经长时间积攒大量泡沫,未来是否有崩盘的危险。或许等疫情过后,我们才能发现,哪里的房子有泡沫,哪里的房子才是真金白银。

星环集团
STAR RING GROUP

星环集团 STAR RING

移民　留学　教育　旅游

诚信赢天下

604-370-6618

星环移民
- ◆ **ICCRC持牌顾问+高学历团队**，多对一团队服务模式
- ◆ 全程规划，留学、就业、移民一体化服务
- ◆ 量身定制最优方案，成功率几近100%

星环留学
- ◆ 中小学\大学\研究生留学移民
- ◆ 陪读父母转学签及移民
- ◆ 旅游签转学签
- ◆ 学校申请、学签办理、续签、就业指导及推荐
- ◆ 护工\飞行员留学移民

星环教育
- ◆ 北美教育资源研究与中加职业教育对接
- ◆ **VIP保障式教育**：独创项目，确保入读世界名校，目前成功率100%
- ◆ 留学生教辅、就业与移民一站式解决

星环冠君旅游
- ◆ **加拿大小众之旅**：原住民深度游、艺术之旅、商务/高尔夫/滑雪/游学营、高端包机游、小众定制游等特色项目
- ◆ 特色夏/冬令营
- ◆ 数十年北美旅游业经验，北美旅游牌照齐备

● 全面专业的一站式服务
● 行业领先，成功案例云集
● 中加资源丰富

加拿大星环集团专注于加拿大移民、留学、教育、旅游等业务，资深专家团队精心服务，成功率业内首屈一指。

公司网址：www.starringca.com
总部地址：304-4940 No.3 Road, Richmond, BC, Canada, V6X 3A5

FX168 财经集团

FX168全球投资
不止一位顾问专家：

· 学习有投资百科
· 咨询有持牌团队
· 配置有全球资源

加拿大留学　工作　移民
直 通 车

从答疑解惑到专业定制全程助您！

FX168北美分站：https://www.fx168.ca/
FX168全球投资官网：http://invest.fx168.com/
FX168全球投资专线：021-5382 3500

FX168全球投资公众号　　FX168北美公众号